Getting Started

With

Microsoft Office 4.2

Integrating Applications

Getting Started With Microsoft Office 4.2 Integrating Applications

Babette Kronstadt
Sylvia Russakoff
Lynn Marie Bacon
Pace Computer Learning Center
School of Computer Science and Information Systems
Pace University

Babette Kronstadt
David Sachs
Series Editors
Pace Computer Learning Center
School of Computer Science and Information Systems
Pace University

JOHN WILEY & SONS, INC.
New York / Chichester / Brisbane / Toronto / Singapore

Trademark Acknowledgments:

Microsoft is a registered trademark of Microsoft Corporation
Excel for Windows is a trademark of Microsoft Corporation
Word for Windows is a trademark of Microsoft Corporation
PowerPoint for Windows is a trademark of Microsoft Corporation
Microsoft Office is a trademark of Microsoft Corporation
Windows is a trademark of Microsoft Corporation
Microsoft Access is a registered trademark of Microsoft Corporation
1-2-3 is a registered trademark of Lotus Development Corporation
WordPerfect is a registered trademark of WordPerfect Corporation
IBM is a registered trademark of International Business Machines Corporation
Paradox is a registered trademark of Borland International, Inc.

Portions of this text were adapted from other texts in this series and from Pace University Computer Learning Center manuals.

ISBN 0-471-13553-4

Printed in the United States of America

10 9 8 7 6 5 4 3 2 1

Preface

Getting Started with Microsoft Office 4.2: Integrating Applications provides a step-by-step, hands-on introduction to sharing data among the programs of the Microsoft Office suite of applications. It is designed for students who have a working knowledge of the PC, Windows, *Word for Windows*, and *Excel*. Additional projects are included for students whose knowledge extends to *PowerPoint* and/or *Access*. Each lesson presents carefully structured material, organized in short, focused activities which build to help the student absorb both conceptual and practical knowledge.

Key Elements

Each lesson in *Getting Started with Microsoft Office 4.2: Integrating Applications* uses eight key elements to help students master specific concepts and skills and develop the ability to apply them.

- **Learning objectives**, located at the beginning of each lesson, focus students on the skills to be learned.
- **Project orientation** allows the students to meet the objectives while creating a real-world application. Skills are developed as they are needed to complete projects, not to follow menus or other artificial organization.
- **Motivation** for each activity is supplied so that students learn *why* and *when* to perform an activity, rather than how to follow a series of instructions by rote.
- **Bulleted lists of step-by-step general procedures** introduce the tasks and provide a handy, quick reference.
- **Activities with step-by-step instructions** guide students as they apply the general procedures to solve the problems presented by the projects.
- **Screen displays** provide visual aids for learning and illustrate major steps.
- **Independent projects** provide opportunities to practice newly acquired skills with decreasing level of support.
- **Feature reference** offers students a one page chart organizing and reinforcing the major concepts presented in the book.

Stop and Go

The steps for completing each feature introduced in this book are covered twice. First they are described in a bulleted list, which can be used for reference. Then the same steps are used in a hands-on Activity. **Be sure to wait until the Activity to practice each feature on the computer.**

Flexible Use

Getting Started with Microsoft Office 4.2: Integrating Applications is designed for use in an introductory computer course. As a "getting started" book, it does not attempt to cover all of the possibilities for integrating applications. Rather, it introduces and reinforces the basic methods of application integration that students will be likely to find valuable. While designed to be used in conjunction with lectures or other instructor supervision, concepts are explained clearly enough so that students can use the book in independent learning settings. Students should be able to follow specific instructions with minimal instructor assistance.

Data Disk

Data disks are provided to instructors for distribution to students. The projects use files from the disk so that the lessons can focus on the new skills being learned. Some data entry is always included so that students understand the full application they are building.

Acknowledgments

Getting Started with Microsoft Office 4.2: Integrating Applications was written by three of us, but it represents the work and effort of many individuals and organizations. Nancy Treuer and Matthew Poli performed their usual miracles with the layout and text formatting. Jessica Kronstadt was a tremendous help to us by annotating the pictures and working on the index. The files of the fictitious Powell Community Orchestra, which consititute the theme of this book, are based on actual documents from the files of the Chappaqua Chamber Orchestra, Chappaqua, New York. We thank Robert M. Brown for allowing us to base some of our documents on ones he has written.

We received enormous institutional support from Pace University and the School of Computer Science and Information Systems (CSIS) and its Dean, Dr. Susan Merritt.

From another perspective, this book is also a product of the Pace Computer Learning Center, a loose affiliation of approximately 15 faculty and staff who have provided more than 7,000 days of instruction to over 60,000 individuals in corporate settings throughout the United States and around the world during the past nine years. Our shared experiences in the development and teaching of these non-credit workshops, as well as credit bearing courses through the Pace University School of Computer Science and Information Systems, was an ideal preparation for writing this book. In addition none of our books for John Wiley would have been possible without the continuing support of David Sachs, the director of the Computer Learning Center.

We have received many invaluable comments and suggestions from instructors at other schools who were kind enough to review earlier books in the *Getting Started* series and offer their suggestions for the current books. Our thanks go to Jack D. Cundiff, Horry-Georgetown Technical College; Pat Fenton, West Valley College; Sharon Ann Hill, University of Maryland; E. Gladys Norman, Linn-Benton Community College; and Barbara Jean Silvia, University of Rhode Island.

Our thanks also go to the many people at John Wiley who provided us with support and assistance. Our editor, Beth Lang Golub, and editorial program assistant, Christopher Actis, have been very responsive to our concerns, and supportive of all of the Pace Computer Learning Center's writing projects. Andrea Bryant was invaluable in her management of all aspects of the production of this book.

Last but not least, we would like to thank our families without whose support and patience we could not have written this book.

Babette Kronstadt
Sylvia Russakoff
Lynn Marie Bacon

July, 1995
White Plains, New York

Contents

Students and Instructors

Before Getting Started Please Note:

KNOWLEDGE OF MICROSOFT OFFICE APPLICATIONS

Getting Started with Microsoft Office 4.2: Integrating Applications is an introduction to object linking and embedding and other techniques which use two or more of the Office applications together to create documents. This book therefore assumes that students are familiar with the basic commands in *Microsoft Word 6.0 for Windows* and *Microsoft Excel 5.0 for Windows.* These commands are covered in *Getting Started with Microsoft Word 6.0 for Windows* and *Getting Started with Microsoft Excel 5.0, for Windows,* also published by John Wiley & Sons, Inc. In addition, Independent Projects which involve the use of *PowerPoint* or *Access* assume mastery of basic skills in these programs which can be acquired through the use of *Getting Started with PowerPoint 4.0* and *Getting Started with Microsoft Access 2.0 for Windows.*

STUDENT DATA DISKS

Most of the projects in this book require the use of a Data Disk. Instructors who have adopted this text are granted the right to distribute the files on the Data Disk to any student who has purchased a copy of the text. Instructors are free to post the files to standalone workstations or a network or provide individual copies of the disk to students. This book assumes that students who use their own disk know the name of the disk drive that they will be using it from. When using a network, students must know the name(s) of the drives and directories which will be used to open and save files.

SETUP OF WINDOWS AND MICROSOFT OFFICE FOR WINDOWS

One of the strengths of Windows and the applications that comprise Microsoft Office is the ease with which the screens and even some of the programs' responses to commands can be customized. This, however, can cause problems for students trying to learn how to use the programs. This book assumes that Windows, the Microsoft Office Manager and each of the component programs of Office — *Word, Excel, PowerPoint* and *Access* — have been installed using the default settings and that they have not been changed by those using the programs. Some hints are given about where to look if the computer responds differently from the way it would under standard settings. If your screen look different from those in the book, ask your instructor or laboratory assistant to check that the defaults have not been changed.

VERSION OF THE SOFTWARE

All of the screenshots in this book have been taken using Version 4.2 of Microsoft Office. This includes version 6.0 of *Word for Windows,* Version 5.0 of *Microsoft Excel for Windows,* and Version 4.0 of *PowerPoint.* All screenshots of *Access* were taken using Version 2.0, which is part of Microsoft Office Professional, Version 4.3. If you are not using these versions, the appearance of your screen and the effect of some commands may vary slightly from those used in this book.

Introduction

Objectives

In this lesson you will learn how to:

- Define a "suite" of applications
- Understand the advantages of using a suite of applications
- Define "integrating" applications
- Understand the Microsoft Office Manager
- Start the Microsoft Office Manager
- Customize the Microsoft Office Toolbar

This book will follow the format of the other books in the Getting Started series. Except for the Introduction, each lesson will contain a Project (completed in units called Activities), a Summary, Key Terms, and Independent Projects. This book will not repeat material covered in other books of the series. Therefore, students are expected to be familiar with Microsoft Windows 3.1, *Word for Windows*, and *Excel*, and be comfortable using the mouse. Projects in other books of the series are sometimes mentioned, but are not necessary for understanding this book. Independent Projects involve the use of *Access* and *PowerPoint*, for students who wish to integrate these applications with *Word* and/or *Excel*.

WHAT IS A "SUITE" OF APPLICATIONS?

Microsoft Office is considered to be a "suite" of applications. A suite of applications is a group of programs that are purchased, installed, and used together. Although the programs that make up a suite can be bought and run as separate entities, their strength as a suite lies in their ability to work effectively together. Microsoft Office version 4.2 includes a word processing program, *Word for Windows*; a spreadsheet program, *Excel*; and a presentation program, *PowerPoint*. In Microsoft Office Professional (version 4.3), a database program, *Access,* is also included The CD ROM version of Microsoft Office includes *Bookshelf*, a selection of reference materials. The network version includes a message and file sharing program, *Microsoft Mail*. This book is based on the standard version 4.2 of Microsoft Office, but also includes some projects using *Access*.

When you install and use Microsoft Office, all its programs are available to you simultaneously. You are limited only by your hardware (memory and storage space) in regard to how many programs and documents may run at one time.

What Advantages Do You Gain by Using a Suite of Applications?

First, using software from a suite gives you the greatest ease in transferring data from one application to another. Although the Windows environment allows you to transfer data among almost all programs, the applications in a suite are designed to receive each other's information with a minimum of trouble.

Second, you can learn the applications in a suite quickly because the screens and programs resemble each other. Not only do they contain the Windows standard requirements in terms of menu commands and basic operations, they also present a consistent "look" and "feel" and contain many of the same keyboard commands, buttons, and other shortcuts. The degree to which the applications resemble each other varies from suite to suite.

Third, you can think of a suite's features in total, rather than application by application. Because of the easy transfer of data, you can move your information to whichever program has the feature you need at the moment. For example, you can move your data from the database to the spreadsheet if the database in your suite cannot perform the calculations you need and the spreadsheet can.

The compatibility of the applications in a suite is based on all these factors. Although Microsoft Office is only one of several popular suites currently available, it has received top evaluations with regard to its consistency of appearance and ability to handle and transfer information between applications.

What Does Integration of Applications Mean?

Microsoft Corporation has provided a number of features that enable you to use the suite's applications together. Using these features to obtain the most power from your software is called "integrating" your applications. This book will discuss the techniques with which you can integrate two or more applications, combining the strengths of each. These techniques will be explained and reinforced throughout this book.

A simple example of integration would involve *copying* and *pasting* part of an *Excel* worksheet into a report created in *Word for Windows*. A more advanced way of integrating applications, called *linking*, enables you to display the worksheet data in one or more *Word* documents, while saving the data in *Excel*. Linking saves time because when you update your data you do it only once — in the original file. The linked files in *Word* can be automatically and accurately updated. Linking files also saves space, because the worksheet file is the only one that actually contains the data.

Another way of integrating applications is to *embed* part of a file created in one application into a different application. For example, if you were creating a presentation in *PowerPoint*, you could choose to embed an *Excel* worksheet in the presentation. The embedded worksheet becomes part of the *PowerPoint* file (a *linked* worksheet does not.) The difference between embedding and simply pasting the worksheet into *PowerPoint* is that the embedded worksheet can be edited using *Excel's* commands. Clicking on the worksheet in *PowerPoint* will bring up the *Excel* toolbar and menu so you can edit the worksheet. Thus, you can use the capabilities of *Excel* and *PowerPoint* together.

Learning to integrate applications will gradually move you from an "application" orientation to a "task" orientation. Instead of thinking about which *application program* you are using, you will think instead about which *task* you need to accomplish. Instead of viewing your documents as "*Word*" or "*Excel*" documents, you will view each document as an aggregate of parts, created with the features of the different applications you use, and assembled in a single file. You will view each application program as a set of tools, to be used freely as you solve problems at your computer.

STARTING MICROSOFT OFFICE

One of the questions asked during installation of Microsoft Office is whether its icon should be placed in the Startup program group, so that Office will run automatically when you open Windows. If this has been done, your Startup group will look like Figure I - 1.

In addition, many computers are set to run Windows automatically when they are turned on. If both these settings are in place, turning on your PC will run both Windows and Microsoft Office.

If this is *not* the case, use the following procedure to run Windows and Office:

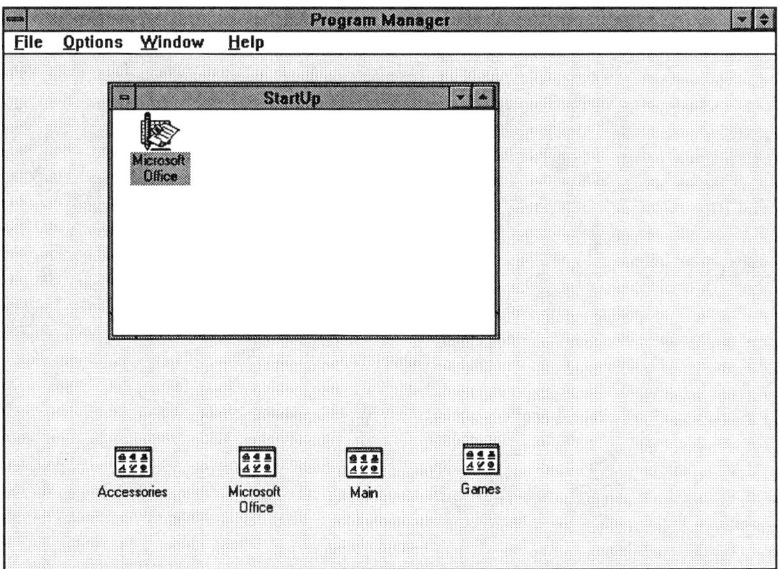

Figure I - 1 Office will start automatically when Windows runs

To run Microsoft Office:

- Turn on the computer and run Windows.
- Open the Microsoft Office program group window.
- Double-click the **Microsoft Office** icon.

  Microsoft Office will open and you will see the Microsoft Office Manager toolbar displayed.

Activity I.1: Starting Microsoft Office

1. Turn on your computer.
2. Run Microsoft Windows 3.1.
3. At the Program Manager, open the Microsoft Office program group window and double-click the **Microsoft Office** icon (Figure I - 2).

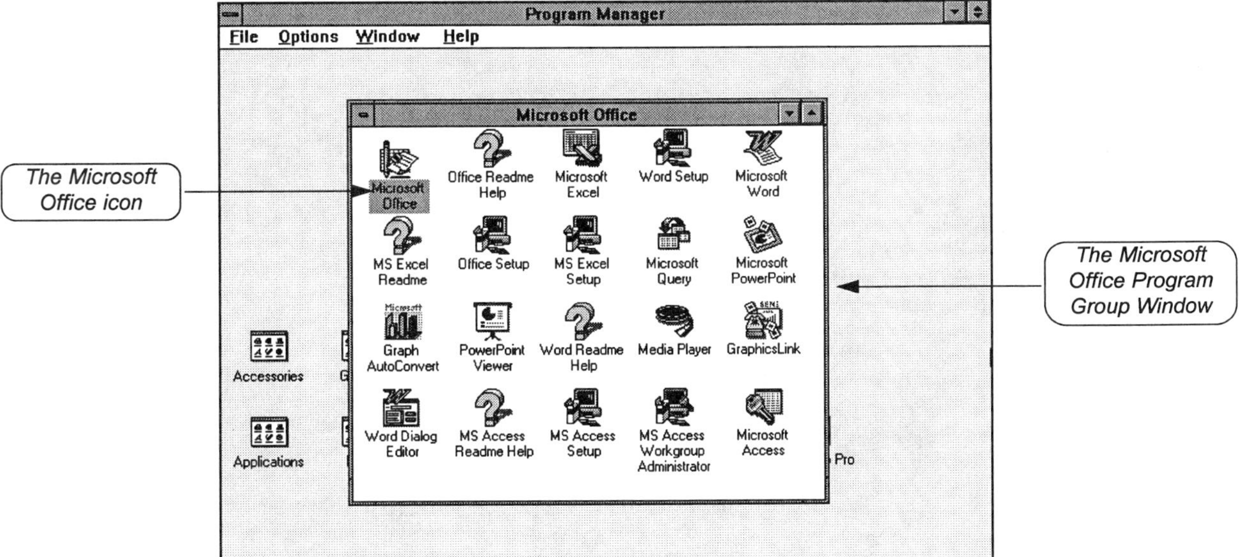

Figure I - 2 Double-click the Microsoft Office icon to run the program

What is the Microsoft Office Manager (MOM)?

The Microsoft Office Manager (MOM) encompasses a variety of tools for using the applications of Microsoft Office. It includes a toolbar that is displayed on the Title Bar of each application, a full drop-down menu of programs and commands, and a shortcut menu. The toolbar contains a button for each Microsoft Office application installed on your computer. Pointing to a button will display its name. The toolbar provides a quick, easy way to open applications and to change from one application to another. The MOM toolbar can be customized to include buttons representing other programs from Windows (for example the File Manager or the Notepad), and other programs you may own that are not part of Microsoft Office. The following figures display examples of how the MOM toolbar may look:

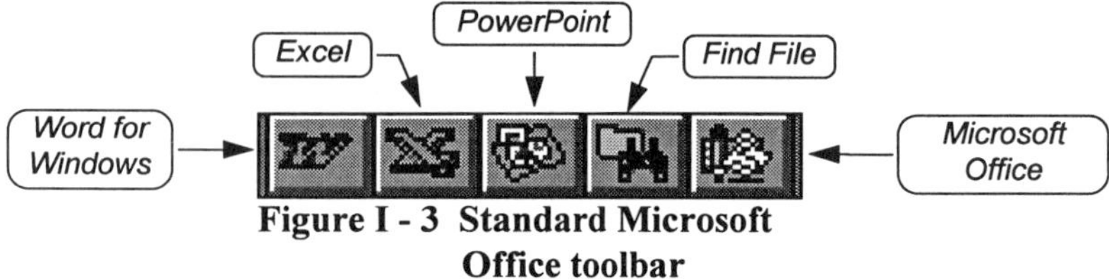

Figure I - 3 Standard Microsoft Office toolbar

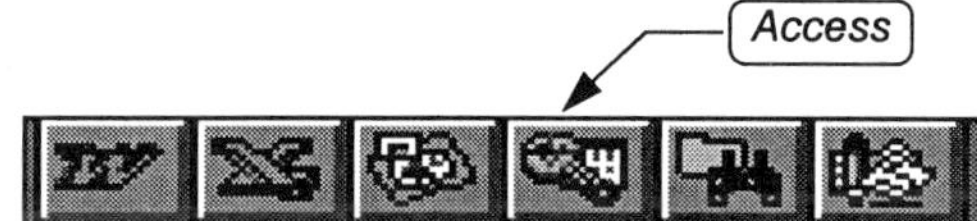

Figure I - 4 Standard toolbar with Access button added

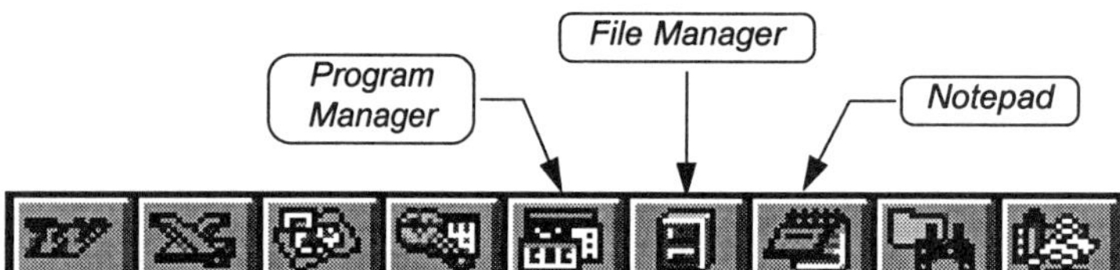

Figure I - 5 Standard toolbar with Access, Program Manager, File Manager and Notepad buttons added

To use the Office Manager toolbar to open or switch applications:

- Point to the button on the Office toolbar that represents the application you want to open or switch to.
- Click the left mouse button.

  The application you have chosen will open, or if it is already open it will become the active application.

The drop-down Microsoft Office menu is opened by clicking the last button on the toolbar. You may choose any option from the menu by clicking on it (Figure 1 - 6).

To use the Microsoft Office Dropdown Menu:

- Point to the **Microsoft Office** button on the Office toolbar and click.
- Choose the application or command of your choice.

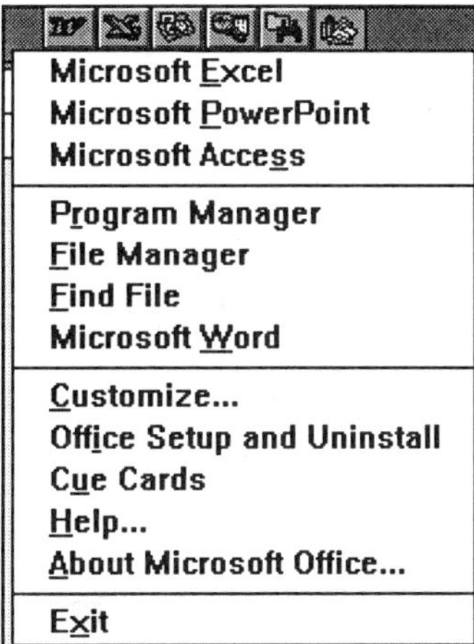

Figure I - 6 The MOM drop-down menu

The shortcut menu is opened by pointing to the Office toolbar and clicking the *right* mouse button. It contains commands for changing the appearance of the Office toolbar (Figure I - 7).

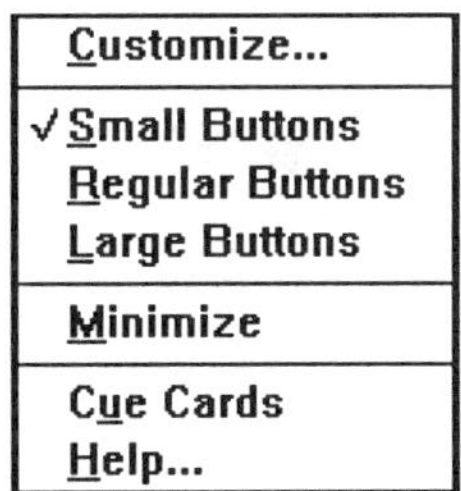

Figure I - 7 The MOM shortcut menu

To use the Microsoft Office shortcut menu:

- Point to a spot anywhere on the Office toolbar.
- Click the *right* mouse button.
- Choose the application or command of your choice.

Activity I.2: Using the Microsoft Office Manager

The following activity will help you become familiar with the MOM toolbar, drop-down menu, and shortcut menu. Your toolbar should contain, at a minimum, the buttons pictured in Figure I -3. If not, speak to the person in charge of your computer room, or read the section about customizing the toolbar at the end of this lesson. Another possibility is that the display of the toolbar has been turned off. Exercise I.3 will show you how to display it permanently.

1. Open Microsoft Office, if it is not already open. For help,see Activity I.1.
2. Rest your mouse arrow on each button of the Office toolbar in turn, reading and noting the name of each.

PROBLEM SOLVER: *If the toolbar is not visible, press **ALT+TAB**. When the Office toolbar appears, click the **MICROSOFT OFFICE** button on the Office toolbar and choose **Customize** from the menu. At the **Customize** dialog box, click on the **View** menu and then place an **X** in the box marked **Toolbar is Always Visible**. Choose **OK**.*

3. To open *Word for Windows*, click the **WORD** button on the Office toolbar.

   Word will open, and you will see the Office toolbar on top of Word's title bar (Figure I - 8).

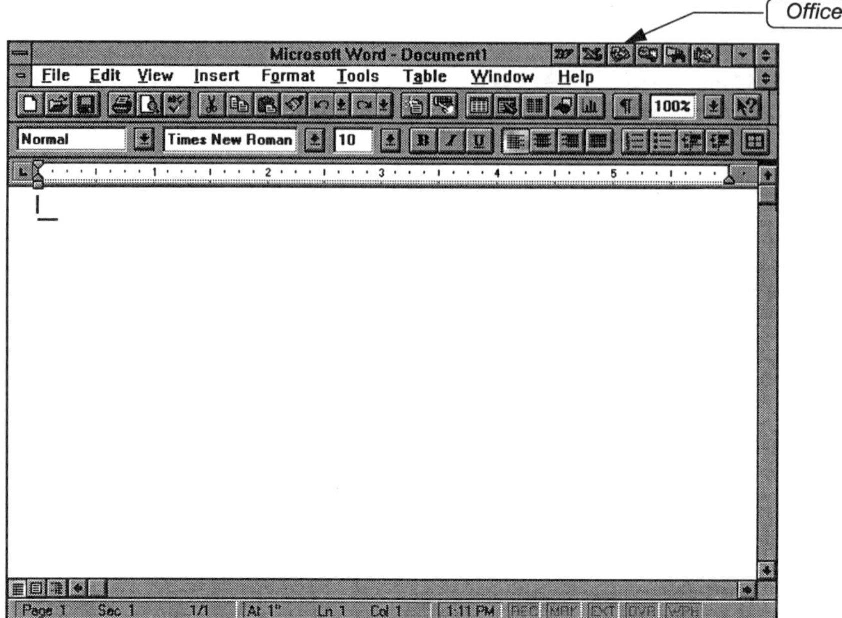

Figure I - 8 The Office toolbar displayed on the *Word for Windows* screen

4. Type your name on the *Word* screen.

5. To change to *Excel*, click the **EXCEL** button on the Office toolbar.
6. Type the date into cell **A1** of *Excel.*

7. To display the drop-down menu, click the **OFFICE** button on the Office toolbar.
8. Click the words **Program Manager** on the menu.

   Even though you reach the Program Manager window, Office keeps running.

9. Click the **WORD** button again to return to *Word.*

   Notice that your name is still there — you have returned to your open Word document.

10. Click the **POWERPOINT** button to run *PowerPoint*. If the **Tip of the Day** dialog box appears, choose **OK**. Choose **Cancel** at the *PowerPoint* Startup dialog box.

   PROBLEM SOLVER: *If PowerPoint has not been installed on your computer it will not run, even though its button may present. If you do not have PowerPoint, skip* ***Step 10****.*

11. Switch back to *Excel* by clicking the **EXCEL** button.
12. Close *Excel* by choosing **FILE/Exit** from the *Excel* menu bar.
13. Answer **No** when you are asked if you wish to save changes.

    You will return to PowerPoint or Word.

14. If *PowerPoint* is open, choose **FILE/Exit** from the *PowerPoint* menu bar.
15. Point to the Office toolbar and click the *right* mouse button to see the shortcut menu.
16. Click the words **Large Buttons** to see how the toolbar buttons look when enlarged.

*When you choose **Large Buttons**, the Office toolbar may move to a different part of the screen. This will not affect your ability to continue with this activity. If the toolbar is no longer visible, follow the **Problem Solver** instructions in **Step 2** to display it.*

17. Exit from *Word* without saving changes.
18. Open the shortcut menu again and return to **Small Buttons**.

    *Changing the buttons back to **Small** will return the toolbar to its original location at the top of the screen. At this point, all applications will be closed, but Office will still be running.*

19. Open the Office drop-down menu, and click on **Exit** to close Office.

Moving and Displaying the Microsoft Office Manager Toolbar

The Office toolbar can be moved, and can be turned on and off whenever you wish. If the toolbar is not showing, it may have been turned off, or else it has been set so that it is not visible at all times. The following instructions and exercise will help you control the size, placement, and visibility of the Office toolbar. You cannot move the toolbar when the button size is set at **Small**, so you will make that change first.

To move the Office toolbar:

- Click the **MICROSOFT OFFICE** button on the Office toolbar.
- Choose the **Customize** command.
- Choose the **View** tab.
- Choose **Regular** or **Large** buttons.

  The change in button size makes it possible to move the toolbar, which now has a Title Bar.

- Click on the toolbar Title Bar to drag the toolbar to a different part of your screen.

  Sometimes the toolbar will move to a different part of the screen without you dragging it.

To turn the Office toolbar off and on:

- To turn off the toolbar, double-click the small control menu box in its upper left corner.

  Turning off the toolbar closes Microsoft Office.

- To turn the toolbar on again, return to the Program Manager and double-click the Microsoft Office icon (for help, see page 3).

  Turning the toolbar back on opens Microsoft Office again.

To control the visibility of the toolbar:

The Office toolbar can be set so that it is always visible, or so that it is visible only when it is active.

- Click the **MICROSOFT OFFICE** button on the Office toolbar.
- Choose the **Customize** command.
- Choose the **View** tab.
- Examine the box marked **Toolbar is Always Visible**.
- Place or remove an **X** in the box.

  *Placing an **X** in the box will mean that the toolbar is always displayed. Removing an **X** from the box will mean that the toolbar is displayed only when it is active.*

- Choose **OK**.
- If you have removed the **X**, when you click on **OK** you may no longer see the Office toolbar. To make the toolbar active, press **ALT+TAB** until you reach **Microsoft Office** and you will be able to see it. Repeat this whenever you need to see the toolbar.

Customizing the Microsoft Office Manager Toolbar

The next activity will teach you how to customize the appearance of the Office toolbar by adding and removing buttons to reflect the programs you use most frequently. If you are using a school or lab computer, take careful note of the toolbar's initial appearance — you will be expected to return the toolbar to this appearance by the conclusion of this activity. The activity assumes that you begin with the standard Office toolbar, containing buttons for *Word*, *Excel*, *PowerPoint*, *Find File*, and *Microsoft Office* (Figure I - 3). If your toolbar is set differently, do as much of the activity as you can. It is possible that your network administrator has set Office so that the toolbar cannot be customized. If so, skip the activity.

To Customize the Office toolbar:

- Click the **MICROSOFT OFFICE** button on the Office toolbar.
- Choose **Customize**.
- Choose the **Toolbar** section of the **Customize** dialog box.
- To add a program to the toolbar, place an **X** in the box preceding its name.
- To remove a program from the toolbar, remove the **X** in the box preceding its name.
- To rearrange the order of buttons on the toolbar, select a program you have checked and use the **Move** button(s) to change its position on the list.
- Choose **OK** when you are done.

Activity I.3: Customizing the Office Toolbar

1. Open Microsoft Office.
2. If you are using a computer that is not your own, write down a list of the current toolbar buttons. You will be expected to return the toolbar to this appearance by the end of the activity.
3. Open the drop-down menu by clicking the **MICROSOFT OFFICE** button on the Office toolbar.
4. Choose **Customize**.

   *The **Customize** dialog box has three tabbed sections: **Toolbar, Menu,** and **View**.*
5. Choose the **Toolbar** tab.

   You will see a list of Microsoft programs, beginning with Office applications and continuing with other Microsoft programs.
6. Scroll down the list and you will see a group of Windows programs, for example *File Manager*, *Paintbrush,* and *Calculator*. By adding one or more of these programs to the Office toolbar, you can reach them easily, without returning to the Windows Program Manager.
7. Scroll to the top of the list and place an **X** in the box in front of **Microsoft Access**.
8. Scroll down and place an **X** in front of **Program Manager** and in front of **File Manager**.

   These programs will be added to the Office toolbar, in the list order.

9. Click **OK** or press **ENTER**. Your toolbar should look like Fig I - 9.

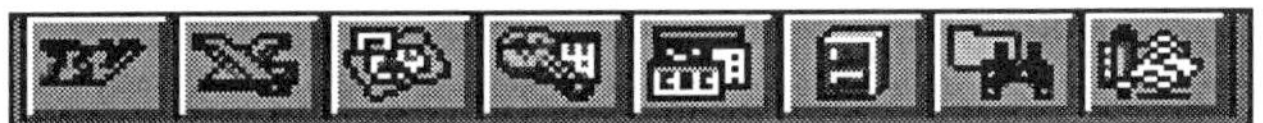

Figure I - 9 A customized Office toolbar

10. Click the **MICROSOFT OFFICE** button, choose **Customize** again, and click on the **View** tab.

    This section allows you to change the size of the toolbar buttons.

11. Choose **Regular** or **Large** buttons. Choose **OK**.
12. On the toolbar, point to the empty space around the buttons, click and drag the toolbar to the middle of your screen.

    *You cannot drag the toolbar if the button size is set to **Small**. When you change the button size, your toolbar may have already moved to a different spot on your screen without your dragging it. This spot is the position chosen by the previous user.*

13. To turn the toolbar off, double-click the control menu in the upper left corner of the toolbar.

    By turning off the Office toolbar, you have closed Microsoft Office

14. Return to the Program Manager and double-click the Microsoft Office icon to run the program again.

    When you reopen the program, the Office toolbar will reappear just where you left it.

15. Drag the toolbar by its Title Bar back up to the upper right corner of the screen.
16. Click the **MICROSOFT OFFICE** button, choose **Customize** and **View** again, and return to **Small** buttons. Choose **OK**.
17. Click the **MICROSOFT OFFICE** button, choose **Customize** and **Toolbar**, and return the Office toolbar to the appearance you recorded in **Step 2** by removing the **X** from each box you you added an **X** to in Steps **7** and **8**. Choose **OK**.
18. Click the **MICROSOFT OFFICE** button, choose **Customize** again, and this time click on the **Menu** section. Examine the screen.

    This section allows you to modify the contents of the drop-down menu in the same way you modified the toolbar.

19. Click on the **View** tab.
20. Remove the **X** in the box marked **Toolbar is Always Visible.** Choose **OK**.

    Now the toolbar may not be visible. Removing the X makes the toolbar visible only when it is the active application. When a different application is active, the toolbar will not show.

21. If the toolbar is not visible, hold down the **ALT** key and tap the **TAB** until you see the words **Microsoft Office** on your screen. Release the **ALT** key. The Office toolbar will be visible.

    *Whenever you need to see the Office toolbar, you may press **ALT+TAB** to make it appear.*

22. To make the toolbar permanently visible again, click the **MICROSOFT OFFICE** button, choose **Customize** and **View**.
23. Replace the **X** in the box marked **Toolbar is Always Visible.** Choose **OK**.

    The toolbar will return to its previous size and location.

24. Click the **MICROSOFT OFFICE** button and choose **Exit** to close the program.

SUMMARY

In the Introduction, we have begun to discuss the concepts that you will be studying throughout this book. We have introduced the ways in which you can share or integrate data among the applications of **Microsoft Office**: *pasting, embedding* and *linking*. We have discussed how these procedures will lead you towards a *task* rather than an *application* orientation to your work at the computer. Finally, we have explored the **Microsoft Office Manager (MOM),** and ways to use and customize the **Microsoft Office** toolbar.

KEY TERMS

Application Orientation
Embedding Applications
Integration
Linking applications
Microsoft Office Manager (MOM)
Microsoft Office Toolbar
Shortcut Menu
Suite
Task Orientation

Lesson

Copying and Pasting

Objectives

In this lesson you will learn how to:

- Begin to differentiate pasting, linking, and embedding data between applications
- Copy data from *Excel* and paste it into *Word*
- Edit and format data copied from *Excel* and pasted into *Word*
- Use *Word*'s **TABLE/Table AutoFormat** command
- Understand the effect of changing data pasted in the destination document on the source document
- Paste *Word* text and *Excel* worksheets and charts into *PowerPoint*
- Copy data from *Excel* and paste it into *Access*

PROJECT DESCRIPTION

Getting Started with Microsoft Word 6.0 for Windows used documents created for the fictional Powell Community Orchestra. In this book, you will use *Word* along with the other programs in Microsoft Office to produce reports, presentations, and other documents for the same orchestra. In this project you, as the orchestra treasurer, need to complete a memo to the Board of Trustees on the success of the latest fundraising drive. The financial data that you need to include in your report exists in the worksheet **fundrais.xls. Fundrais.xls** is complete and you do not expect that any changes to it will be necessary. You don't want to re-type the worksheet data into your memo — and thanks to the compatibility between *Word* and *Excel* you don't need to!

Figure 1 - 1 shows your completed memo. The financial data has been copied from **fundrais.xls** and then formatted in *Word* to match the other table in the memo. As you read in the Introduction, there are several ways that data can be shared between *Excel* and *Word.* Therefore, before actually creating the memo, we'll review the other methods and explain why you are using copy and paste to include the *Excel* data in your *Word* memo.

TO COPY, LINK, OR EMBED?

Windows applications have become popular because they have made using computers easier. All Windows programs have a similar interface — consequently if you learn one application it's easier to learn a second one. Windows applications are also popular because of the ways data can be shared between documents created in different Windows applications. As discussed in the Introduction, it is particularly easy to share data among the Microsoft Office applications.

Memorandum

DATE: July 14, 1995

TO: Board of Directors

FROM: Nancy Logan, Treasurer

RE: 1994-1995 Fundraising

This year's fundraising activities have been our most successful ever. My thanks to the many board members who were actively involved in our fundraising activities. More board members were involved than in previous years and I'm sure that this level of participation was responsible for our success. At Ellen Koff's suggestion, we tried a raffle this year and the results were excellent. My special thanks go to those who took leadership roles in the orchestra's fundraising activities:

Chairperson	Committee	Comments
Jessica Crown	Benefit Concert	The inclusion of dancers from the New York City Ballet was a first for our benefit.
Ellen Koff	Raffle	This is a new event that should be repeated next year.
Gabe State	Corporate Grants	Three new corporate givers were added this year.
Nina Russell	Government/Individual Grants	Government money has become tighter, but at least we have been hurt less than some other organizations.
Matt Lewis	Commissioned Works	Three works were commissioned during the year.

Fundraising contributed 47% of our total revenues this year. We received $3,555 more than last year. The table below shows the distribution of revenue from fundraising activities this year and last.

Fundraising Activity	1993/1994 Revenue	1994/1995 Revenue	Increase/ Decrease	% Increase/ Decrease
Individual Donations				
Trustees	$ 3,750	$ 4,200	$ 450	12%
Non Trustees	3,275	3,325	50	2%
Corporate Donations	1,650	1,850	200	12%
Government Grants	1,500	1,200	(300)	-20%
Benefit Concert	1,395	1,450	55	4%
Raffle		1,100	1,100 (NA)	
Commissioned Works		2,000	2,000 (NA)	
Total	$ 11,570	$ 15,125	$ 3,555	31%

Using these results, I propose that we calculate next year's budget assuming the same percent increase/decrease in all activity areas present in both 1993/1994 and 1994/1995 and a 10% increase in the two new fundraising activities. This proposal is on the agenda for the next board meeting.

Figure 1 - 1 Completed memo

Copying and Pasting Data

The first way to share data is through copying and pasting. As you learned in the *Getting Started* books on *Word* and *Excel*, when you copy data it is placed on the Windows Clipboard, which serves as a temporary storage area for information that you are in the process of copying or moving. Since the clipboard belongs to Windows rather than to *Word* or *Excel*, the information is available not only to the program from which it was copied, but to other Windows programs as well.

The major limitation of copying and pasting data is that the copied information becomes part of the document to which it was copied and retains no connection to the original document or the application used to create it. If you change the original data and you want these same revisions in the copied data, you must recopy the (revised) data. Similarly, the copied data maintains no relationship to the application program in which it was created. Any editing or formatting changes are made using the commands of the application in which it is now contained. For example, if you copy part of an *Excel* worksheet into a *Word* document, the worksheet becomes a *Word* table. You can edit it just as you would any other *Word* table. But if you change one of the copied numbers and that number was included in a calculation in the worksheet, the calculation is not automatically updated in the *Word* table as it would be in *Excel*.

Object Linking and Embedding — More Sophisticated Ways of Sharing Data

Windows has developed a procedure called *OLE (Object Linking and Embedding)* to overcome the limitations of copying and pasting. OLE lets you create an ongoing connection between the data in the new location and the original data or the original application.

Several terms are useful for understanding OLE. The term *object* is used to refer to a set of data, such as part or all of a worksheet, a word, sentence, or several paragraphs from a document, an *Excel* chart, a *PowerPoint* slide, etc. that you create and edit in one application and then insert and store in a different application. (Sometimes the term object is still used if the data is stored in a different document or different part of the same application.) The location of the original object is referred to as the *source document* or *file* and its application is the *source application.* The new location of the pasted, linked or embedded object is the *destination document* in the *destination application.* The data being shared is the *source data.* For example, in Figure 1 - 2 a range from an *Excel* worksheet (the source document) has been copied and pasted into a memo in *Word* (the destination document). *Excel* is the source application and *Word* is the destination application.

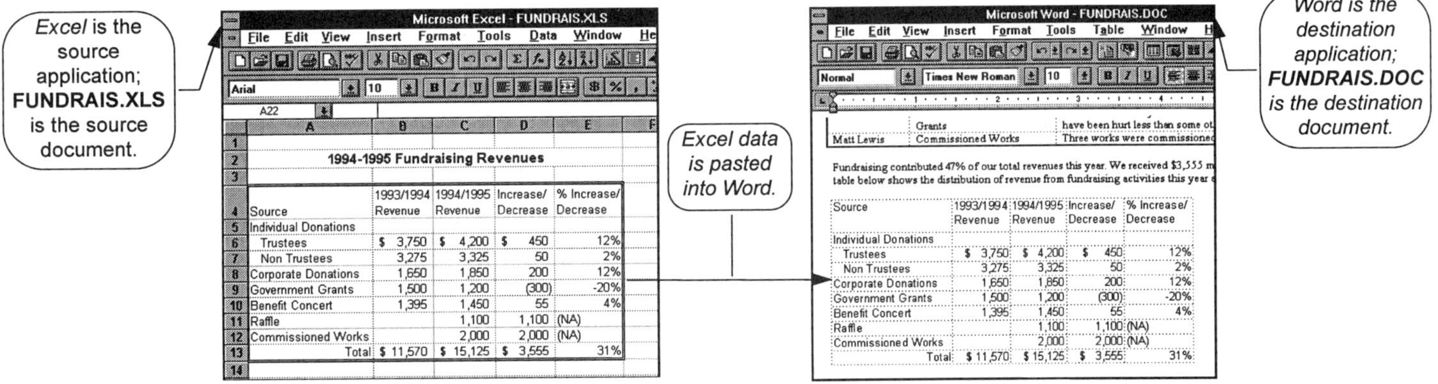

Figure 1 - 2 Data from an *Excel* worksheet (the source document) has been copied into a *Word* memo (the destination document)

Object linking means that the original (source) object and the linked object (in the destination document) are connected so that if you make a change to the source, the destination is aware of the change and can be updated either automatically or at your command.

Object embedding means that the relationship is between the *embedded object* (in the destination document), and the original (source) application rather than the original (source) document. Therefore, the *embedded* object is *not* updated when the *source* (original) object is changed. Instead, when you try to edit an embedded object, the source application is opened and all the commands and capabilities of that application can be used in the editing process.

These are complicated and confusing ideas. Don't worry if you don't understand all the object linking and embedding concepts yet; we'll illustrate them in this and the next two lessons.

Copying and Pasting from fundrais.xls to fundrais.doc

Since linking, embedding, and pasting are different ways to share information between applications, you must decide which way works best in a given situation. In the projects in this and the next two lessons we will analyze each task to see why the method you will be using works. By the time you have completed all three lessons, you should be able to choose the best method yourself.

We'll begin by asking several questions:

- Do I expect the source data to change? If it changes, do I want the data in the destination document to change automatically also?
- Will I need to edit the data once it is in the destination document? If so, do I want to use the source application or the destination application to do the editing?

Let's see how you would answer these questions in our current task. In this project the worksheet information that you want to include in your memo is complete. The memo is going to be distributed to the trustees as soon as it is completed, so even if the worksheet should change later, the memo could not be updated. Once the worksheet data is included in the worksheet, the only change you want to make is to format it like the other table in the memo. Therefore, you want to use *Word*'s (the destination application's) formatting commands to modify the data's appearance, not *Excel*'s (the source application's). This is the perfect situation in which to use copy and paste.

Use copy and paste to share data if:

- The pasted data in the destination document does not need to change if the original data from which it was copied changes.
- You do not want to make any changes to the copied data, or any changes you do make can be made using the commands of the destination application.

OPENING THE SOURCE AND DESTINATION DOCUMENTS

Fundrais.doc on your data disk contains the beginning of your memo to the Board of Trustees of the Powell Community Orchestra. **Fundrais.xls** contains the fundraising worksheet data. You will open and examine both documents first.

Activity 1.1: Opening the Source and Destination Documents

1. Start Microsoft Office, if necessary. Use the Microsoft Office toolbar to open *Word.*
2. Open the file **fundrais.doc** from your data disk.

   Fundrais.doc *is a memo from the orchestra treasurer to the board about the 1994-1995 fundraising activities.*
3. Print the memo. Read it so that you know what it says so far.
4. Press **CTRL+END** to move the cursor to the end of the memo.
5. Type:

   Fundraising contributed 47% of our total revenues this year. We received $3,555 more than last year. The table below shows the distribution of revenue from fundraising activities this year and last.
6. Press **ENTER** twice.

   You are now ready to include the data from your worksheet. Your document should resemble Figure 1 - 3.
7. Use the Office toolbar to switch to *Microsoft Excel.*
8. Open the worksheet file, **fundrais.xls**.

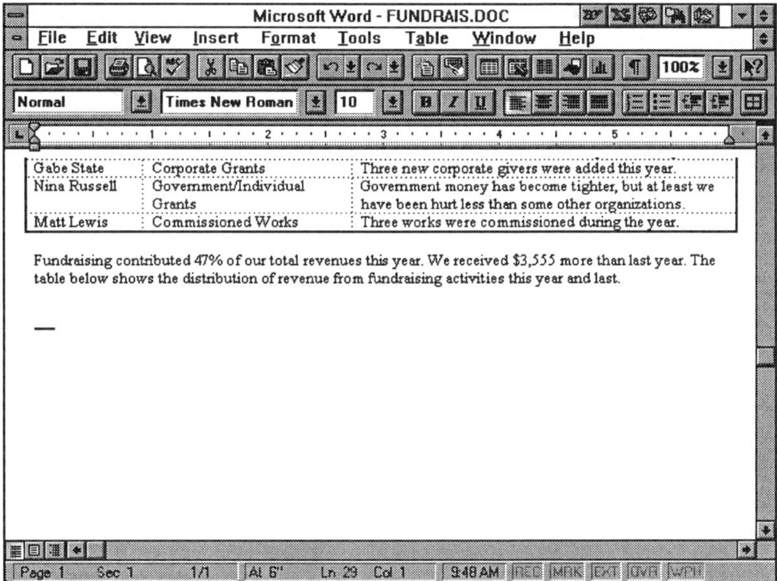

Figure 1 - 3 Memo with newly entered paragraph

COPYING AND PASTING BETWEEN APPLICATIONS

The procedures for copying data from one Office application to another are similar to the procedures you used within an application to copy from one part of the document to another or from one document or worksheet to another. The main difference is that after you copy the data, you must switch to the destination application and document before pasting the data.

To copy data from one application and paste it into another:

- Select the data in the source application.
- Choose **EDIT/Copy** or click on the **COPY** button on the Standard toolbar.
- Activate the destination application by clicking on its button on the Microsoft Office toolbar.
- Open the destination document, if necessary, and move the insertion point to the place at which the data should be pasted.
- Choose **EDIT/Paste** or click on the **PASTE** button on the Standard toolbar.

NOTE: *Most Windows applications have* ***EDIT/Copy*** *and* ***EDIT/Paste*** *commands. Because of the high degree of similarity in the Microsoft Office programs, they even share the same toolbar button for these tasks.*

Activity 1.2: Copying and Pasting Part of an Excel Worksheet into a Word Document

1. Make sure that the worksheet **fundrais.xls** is the active document.
2. Select the range, **A4:E13**.
3. Choose **EDIT/Copy** or click on the **COPY** toolbar button.

   The area to be copied is surrounded by a moving border and the message ***"Select destination and press ENTER or choose Paste"*** *should appear on the Status bar (Figure 1 - 4).*

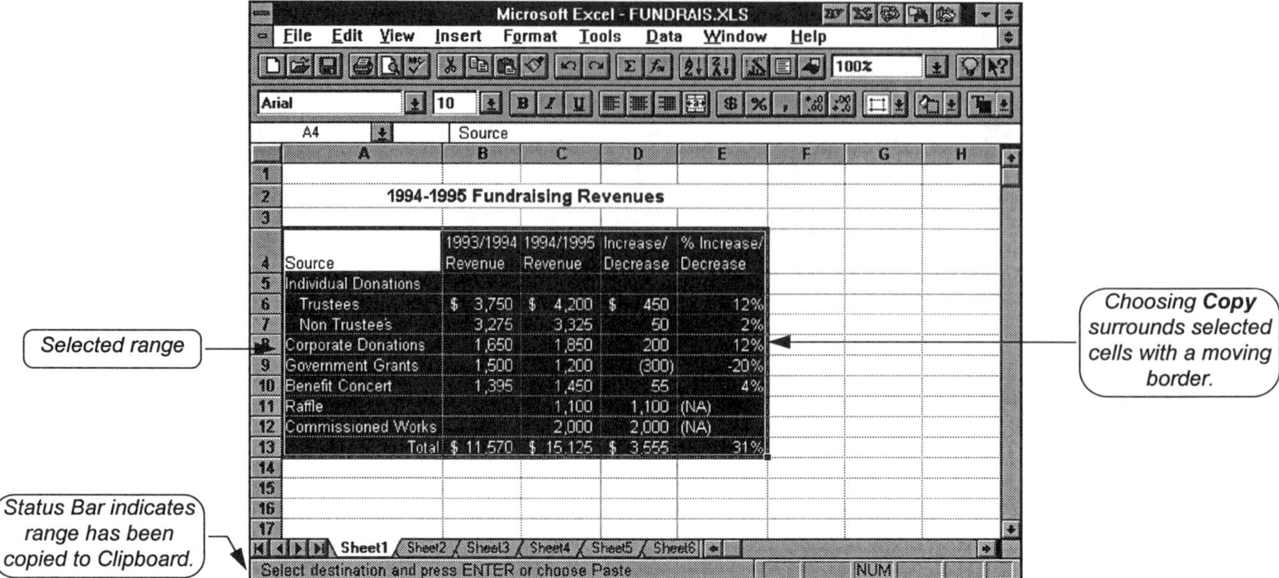

Figure 1 - 4 Fundrais.xls after A4:E13 has been copied to clipboard

4. Switch back to *Word.*

   The insertion point should be at the end of the memo.

5. Choose **EDIT/Paste** or click on the **PASTE** toolbar button.

   The formatted text from the worksheet is inserted into a Word table. Therefore the gridlines appear as the Word default, dotted, nonprinting lines, rather than as the solid printable lines that were in the original Excel worksheet. All values are copied as numbers (constants) even if they were the result of formulas in the Excel worksheet.

6. **Save** the file **as fundrmem.doc** (Figure 1 - 5).

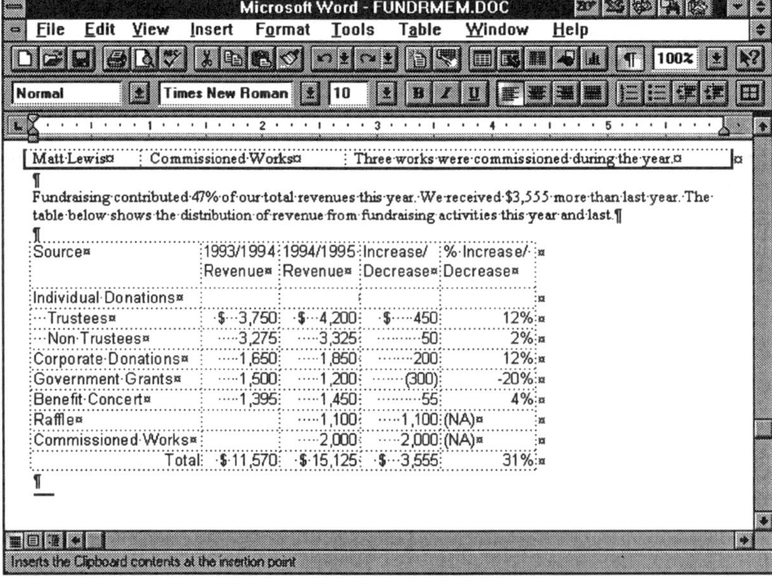

Figure 1 - 5 Fundrais.doc with pasted *Excel* worksheet range

EDITING COPIED AND PASTED DATA

One of the main characteristics of copy and paste is that once the data is pasted in the destination document, there is no further relationship between the data and its source document or application. Therefore, any editing is done using the commands and rules of the destination application.

Following this rule, when part of an *Excel* worksheet is copied and pastec into *Word,* the formatted characters from the worksheet are inserted into a *Word* table because the table format is similar to *Excel*'s column and row format. You can now edit the data exactly as you would in any other *Word* table.

CAUTION: *If you attempt to copy and paste data that cannot be edited using the features of the destination application, the data will automatically be embedded in the destination document instead of just pasted. For example, if you had tried to copy an Excel chart instead of part of an Excel worksheet, when you selected* ***EDIT/Paste*** *Word would have automatically embedded the chart into the memo rather than copied it, because Word cannot edit charts without the help of another program. You'll see how this works when you try to paste an Excel chart into PowerPoint in Independent Activity 1.2. You will learn how to correctly embed and edit embedded objects in Lesson 2.*

Activity 1.3: Editing and Formatting Copied Data

Once the worksheet has been copied into the memo, you decide that you want to make two changes. First, you want to change the column title "Source" to "Fundraising Activity." Second, you want to format the table to match the other table in the memo.

When you formatted tables in *Getting Started with Microsoft Word 6.0 for Windows*, you made each individual formatting change (changing fonts, adding borders, etc.) yourself. *Word* also has a command called **Table AutoFormat**, which offers you different sets of formats that can be applied in one step. We chose one of these autoformats to format the first table, and you will choose the same autoformat to format the part of the worksheet that you just copied and pasted.

1. Click the mouse in the first cell of the embedded worksheet table just before the word *Source*.
2. Use normal *Word* editing procedures to replace the word *Source* with: **Fundraising Activity**
3. Scroll up until you see all of the first table.
4. Click anywhere in the table.

   Examine the formatting of the table. The column titles are in white on a black background and there is a border around the entire chart, but no lines between columns or rows.
5. Choose **TABLE/Table AutoFormat** (Figure 1 - 6).

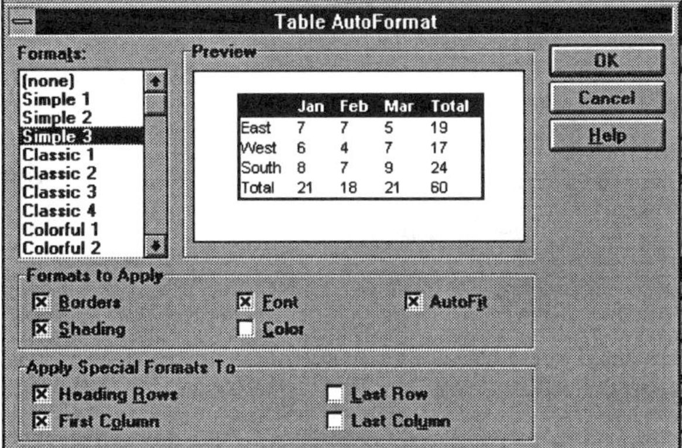

Figure 1 - 6 The Table AutoFormat dialog box for the chairperson table

*The **Table AutoFormat** dialog box should appear. In the **Formats** list box, the format **Simple 3** should be selected and that format should be displayed in the **Preview** area. This format is selected because it is the one applied to the current table. The column titles are in white on a black background and there is a border around the entire chart, but no lines between columns or rows.*

6. Click on **Cancel** to exit the dialog box without changing the format.
7. Scroll down and click anywhere in the table created from the *Excel* worksheet range.
8. Choose **TABLE/Table AutoFormat.**

   *The **Simple 1** format should be selected as that is the first one on the list and no format has yet been applied to this table.*

9. Choose **Simple 3** and click on **OK**.

   *The second table should now be formatted similarly to the first. However, there is a problem. One of the default options in **Table AutoFormat** is **AutoFit,** which should adjust column widths to the widest entry. This did not happen in your table (Figure 1 - 7).*

CAUTION: *Sometimes, when a worksheet range is copied and pasted as a Word table, some of the Excel formatting does not transfer correctly or interferes with Word table formatting commands. Similar problems sometimes occur when data is copied and pasted between other Office applications.*

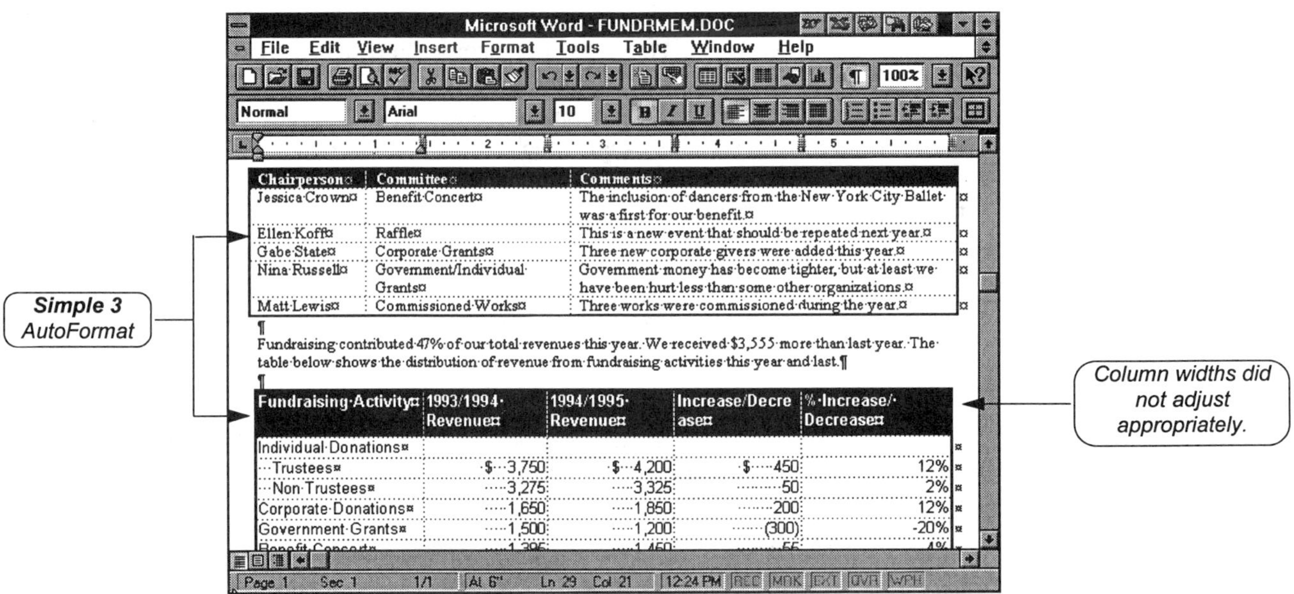

Figure 1 - 7 Problems in applying Table AutoFormat to data pasted from *Excel*

10. You could fix the worksheet table by manually resizing the columns. However, a simpler solution is to undo the format and then reapply it after turning off **AutoFit**. To do this:

    a. Make sure the mouse pointer in still in the second table.

    b. Choose **EDIT/Undo AutoFormat** or click on the **UNDO** button once.

PROBLEM SOLVER*: If **Undo AutoFormat** does not appear on the **Edit** menu, click on the down arrow next to the **UNDO** button and click on **AutoFormat**.*

    c. Choose **TABLE/Table AutoFormat.**

    d. Unmark the **AutoFit** check box so that it will not be applied in the format you choose.

e. Choose **Simple 3** again (Figure 1 - 8) and click on **OK**.

*The **Simple 3** format is applied, but the column widths are not changed.*

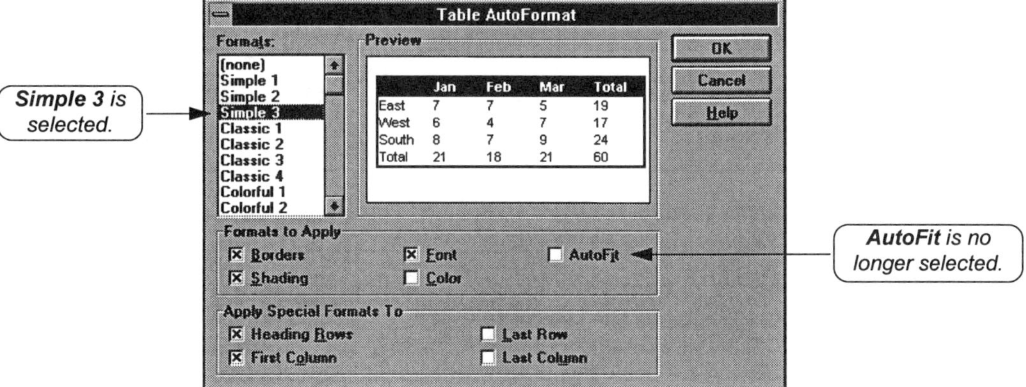

Figure 1 - 8 The corrected AutoFormat dialog box

11. Press **CTRL+END** and press **ENTER** once to position the insertion point for the last paragraph in the memo.
12. Type the final paragraph of the memo:

    Using these results, I propose that we calculate next year's budget assuming the same percent increase/decrease in all activity areas present in both 1993/1994 and 1994/1995 and a 10% increase in the two new fundraising activities. This proposal is on the agenda for the next board meeting.

13. Check the spelling in the document. Assume that all of the proper names have been spelled correctly (Figure 1 - 9).

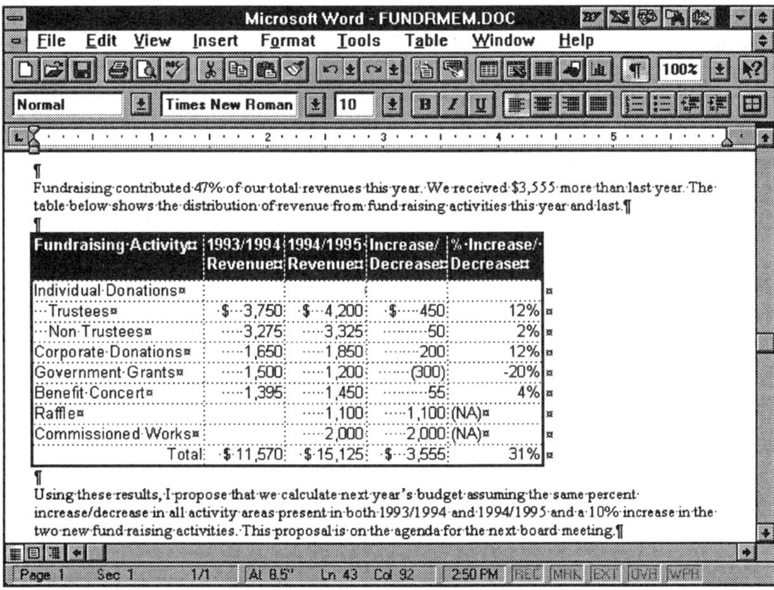

Figure 1 - 9 Your additions to fundrais.doc

14. Save the document using its existing name.
15. Print the document.
16. Close the document.

HOW DID EDITING CHANGES AFFECT THE SOURCE DOCUMENT?

Since there is no continuing relationship between data that has been copied and pasted and its source document, editing changes made to the source do not affect the copied data, and changes made to the copied data do not affect the source data.

Activity 1.4: Seeing the Effect of Your Editing Changes on the Source Data and Vice Versa

First you will return to the *Excel* worksheet to see what, if any, effect your changes to the pasted data had on the source data. Then you will edit the worksheet and see what effect changing the source data has on the pasted data. You will do similar activities in Lessons 2 and 3 after you have linked and embedded worksheet ranges from *Excel* into *Word* so that you can see the different effects of each of these procedures.

In this activity the change you will make to the source document is minor — it will not change the meaning of the worksheet data, so it does not matter that the memo to the trustees has already been sent. If you make any important changes to source data that has been copied and pasted into another document, you must recopy the data or make the same changes to the data in the destination document.

1. Switch to *Excel.*
2. Press **ESC** to remove the moving border from around the range that you copied. Click in **A4**.

   *The title for column **A** remains Source rather than Fundraising Activity as it now appears in the Word document. None of the formatting changes made in Word appear in Excel.*
3. In cell **A11** change *Raffle* to: **Spring Raffle**
4. Save and close the file.
5. Switch back to *Word.* Open **fundrmem.doc**.

   *The change made to **fundrais.xls** is not reflected in the memo.*
6. Close **fundrmem.doc**.
7. Continue with Independent Project 1.1 or exit from *Word* and *Excel.*

SUMMARY

In this lesson you have learned more about ways of sharing information between different Microsoft Office applications and have practiced one of these methods — copying and pasting. Copying and pasting is a useful way to avoid reentering information that already exists in another document or application when it is not important that the pasted data have any continuing connection to the source data or application. Anyone who has a copy of the destination file can edited the pasted data even if they do not have access to the application in which it was created. You also saw one problem with cutting and pasting — since *Word* (or any other destination application) handles formatting differently than *Excel* (or any other source application), there are sometimes problems with the way in which the pasted data is formatted or responds to formatting commands in *Word (*the destination application).

Independent Project 1.1 lets you practice copy and paste by copying data from *Excel* and pasting it into *Word* and also lets you see that the same data can be pasted into more than one document. Independent Project 1.2 lets you see that you can copy and paste information from *Word* to *PowerPoint* as easily as from *Excel* to *Word,* but also has a surprise for you. When you copy text from *Word* to *PowerPoint,* the text can be edited in *PowerPoint* using *PowerPoint* commands as you would expect. However, if you try to copy a chart from *Excel* and paste it into *PowerPoint, PowerPoint* will automatically embed rather than paste the chart. The reason for this is simple — when data is pasted into a document in a different application, it can be edited only by using the commands of the destination application. *PowerPoint* does not have the commands to edit charts (without going into another program), so it is smart enough to automatically embed the chart. This enables you to use *Excel* to edit the chart without having to leave *PowerPoint*! You'll learn how to embed objects intentionally in Lesson 2. Independent Project 1.3 lets you copy data from *Excel* and paste it into *Access*.

KEY TERMS

AutoFormat	Embedding	Source Application
Clipboard	Linking	Source Data
Destination Application	Object	Source Document
Destination Document	OLE	Source File

INDEPENDENT PROJECTS

Independent Project 1.1: Copying Worksheet Data from Excel and Pasting It into Two Word Documents

For this project you will leave the orchestra and look at Dan's Sport Shop. You may recognize some of the data as being similar to that found in some of the *Getting Started with Microsoft Excel 5.0 for Windows* projects. In this project you are writing memos to two people about Dan's second quarter sales. The files **danmemo.doc** and **almamem.doc** are *Word* documents containing the beginnings of two memos on the second quarter sales. A third file (**regsales.xls**) is an *Excel* workbook containing three sheets — **2nd Quarter** (which contains the sales figures that you want to use in both memos), **Yearly** (which you will not use at all), and **1st Quarter** (which contains data that you will use in **almamem.doc**). You will see that the same data may be pasted into more than one document. You will also make editing/formatting changes to the data. When completed your documents should resemble Figure 1 - 10 and Figure 1 - 11 although the table formatting in your document may be different than the ones we chose.

MEMORANDUM

TO: DAN WHITE
Manager, Dan's Sport Shop, Inc.

FROM: LAURA MICHAELS
Financial Advisor

RE: Preliminary Second Quarter Regional Sales Figures.

I've just finished my preliminary look at the second quarter regional sales figures and thought you would want to see them right away. I focused on the Northern region as you requested. The table below includes the sales figures summarized by product and region.

PRODUCT	EASTERN	WESTERN	NORTHERN	SOUTHERN	TOTAL
Baseball Bats	$10,500	$5,467	$7,000	$6,000	$28,967
Golf Club Sets	9,975	7,555	7,000	9,887	$34,417
Kayaks	3,500	9,999	7,221	9,600	$30,320
Tennis Racquets	6,522	6,700	17,000	7,700	$37,922
Boxing Gloves	8,800	1,234	3,300	6,600	$19,934
Scuba Gear	8,330	5,200	7,300	9,900	$30,730
Totals	$47,627	$36,155	$48,821	$49,687	$182,290

The highest sales were for tennis racquets in the Northern region. Other items in that region did not sell as well as in other regions. I propose that we conduct a small market research survey to see which of the other product lines should be doing better than they are in this region. I am asking Sue Miller to put together a market research plan and forward it to you.

Figure 1 - 10 The completed memo to Dan White

MEMORANDUM

TO: ALMA ROSE
Manager, Regional Subdivisions
Sports Land, Inc.

FROM: LAURA MICHAELS
Financial Advisor

RE: First/Second Quarter Regional Sales Comparison for Dan's Sport Shop

I have just received preliminary second quarter regional sales figures for Dan's Sport Shop. I have forwarded these figures plus a suggestion for a market research study in the Northern region to Dan. The market research results should give us some ideas on how to increase the sales of other products to the relative level of tennis racquets. The table below includes the sales figures summarized by product and region.

PRODUCT	EASTERN	WESTERN	NORTHERN	SOUTHERN	ACTUAL TOTAL
Baseball Bats	$10,500	$5,467	$7,000	$6,000	$28,967
Golf Club Sets	9,975	7,555	7,000	9,887	$34,417
Kayaks	3,500	9,999	7,221	9,600	$30,320
Tennis Racquets	6,522	6,700	17,000	7,700	$37,922
Boxing Gloves	8,800	1,234	3,300	6,600	$19,934
Scuba Gear	8,330	5,200	7,300	9,900	$30,730
Totals	$47,627	$36,155	$48,821	$49,687	$182,290

Below are sales figures for the 1st quarter. As you can see sales are up overall, but by a very small amount (approximately 2.6%). This is less than the corporate goal of a yearly 5% increase. I suggest that you schedule a meeting with Dan and representatives of the marketing department to plan a new marketing strategy for Dan's shop.

PRODUCT	EASTERN	WESTERN	NORTHERN	SOUTHERN	ACTUAL TOTAL
Baseball Bats	$10,256	$4,567	$6,594	$5,619	$27,036
Golf Club Sets	9,876	7,538	6,748	9,876	$34,038
Kayaks	3,456	9,753	6,729	9,543	$29,481
Tennis Racquets	6,754	6,704	16,789	7,629	$37,876
Boxing Gloves	8,734	1,678	3,489	6,748	$20,649
Scuba Gear	7,890	4,593	6,923	9,145	$28,551
Totals	$46,966	$34,833	$47,272	$48,560	$177,631

Figure 1 - 11 The completed memo to Alma Rose

1. Start Microsoft Office, if necessary. Use the Microsoft Office toolbar to open *Word.*
2. From your data disk, open **danmemo.doc**. Read the beginning of the memo.
3. Press **CTRL+END** to move the insertion point to the end of the memo.
4. Use the Microsoft Office toolbar to open *Excel.*
5. Open **regsales.xls.** The **2nd Quarter** tab should be active. Look over the sales figures for the four regions.
6. Select the range **A8:F15**.
7. Copy the selected range and paste it at the end of **danmemo.doc.**

CAUTION: *Do not copy or cut anything else until you finish this project. Only one set of data can remain on the Windows clipboard at a time. Therefore, if you cut or copy something else it will replace the **regsales.xls** range on the clipboard. You will be pasting the data that you just pasted into a second memo, so you must be careful not to cut or copy anything else until you finish Step 18.*

8. Press **ENTER** once to leave a blank line after the table.

9. Type:

   The highest sales were for tennis racquets in the Northern region. Other items in that region did not sell as well as in other regions. I propose that we conduct a small market research survey to see which of the other product lines should be doing better than they are in this region. I am asking Sue Miller to put together a market research plan and forward it to you.

10. Spell check the memo.
11. **Save** the document **As: 2ndqdan.doc**
12. Make one editing and one formatting change to the data that you copied from *Excel*:
    - Delete the word **actual** from the title of the last column.
    - Use **TABLE/Table AutoFormat** to apply a format of your choice to the worksheet data.
13. Save the document again using the current name.
14. Print the document.

    Your document should resemble Figure 1 - 10 although the table formatting may differ.

15. Close **2ndqdan.doc**.
16. Open the *Word* file, **almamem.doc**.

    This is another memo from Laura Michaels about the data in ***regsales.xls****.*

17. Read the memo and then press **CTRL+END** to move the insertion point to the end of the memo.
18. Choose **EDIT/Paste** or click on the **PASTE** button.
19. The same range of regional sales from **regsales.xls** will be pasted into this memo.

PROBLEM SOLVER: *If you cut or copied something else since you copied the range from* ***regsales.xls****, the data you last cut or copied will have been pasted into* ***almamem.doc****. To correct this mistake, choose* ***EDIT/Undo Paste*** *and follow steps 4 through 7 to copy and paste the range from* ***regsales.xls****.*

20. **Save** the memo **As: alma2.doc**
21. Press **ENTER**.
22. Type:

    Below are sales figures for the 1st quarter. As you can see sales are up overall, but by a very small amount (approximately 2.6%). This is less than the corporate goal of a yearly 5% increase. I suggest that you schedule a meeting with Dan and representatives of the marketing department to plan a new marketing strategy for Dan's shop.

23. Press **ENTER** twice.
24. Switch to *Excel*.
25. Click on the **1st Quarter** tab. This worksheet is similar to the previous one, but contains sales figures for the first quarter.
26. Select the range **A8:F15**.
27. Copy the selected range and paste it at the end of **alma2.doc**.
28. Save the memo again using the current name.
29. Use **TABLE/Table AutoFormat** to apply a format of your choice to each worksheet table. Use the same format for both worksheets.

HINT: *After formatting the first table, move your cursor anywhere in the second table and choose* ***EDIT/Repeat AutoFormat****.*

30. Spell check the document.

31. Save the memo again using the current name.
32. Print the memo.
33. Close **alma2.doc**. Exit from *Word.*
34. Switch to *Excel*, if necessary. Close **regsales.xls** and exit from *Excel.*

Independent Project 1.2: Copying Selected Items from Word and Excel and Pasting Them into PowerPoint

The president of the orchestra has come to you asking for help in creating a presentation that describes the history of the orchestra. Because you are a loyal fan of the orchestra, you are delighted to help. The president has a disk with three files on it. The first file (**history.doc**) is a *Word* document describing the history of the orchestra. The second file (**attend.xls**) is an *Excel* worksheet with a chart showing the attendance at orchestra concerts since the orchestra's inception. The third file (**history.ppt**) is the beginning of a *PowerPoint* presentation. To create the presentation you need to copy selected information from the *Word* document and the *Excel* worksheet to the *PowerPoint* presentation. The procedure you will use is the same as you used to copy data from *Excel* and paste it into *Word.* Then you will use *PowerPoint*'s commands to make editing and formatting changes to the pasted text. When finished slides 2, 4 and 5 of your presentation will resemble Figure 1 - 12, Figure 1 - 13, and Figure 1 - 14.

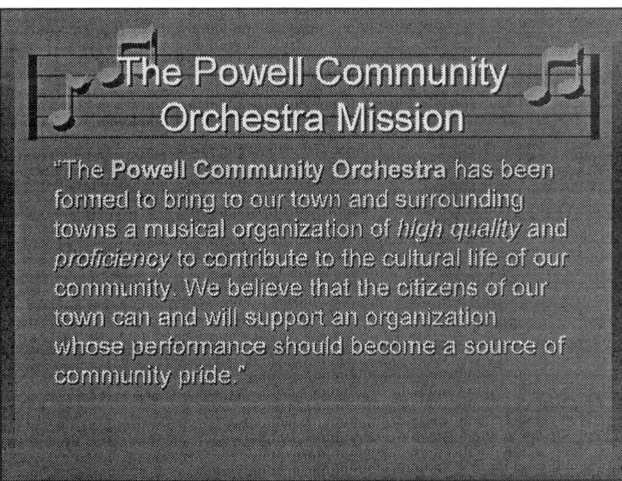

Figure 1 - 12 Completed Slide 2

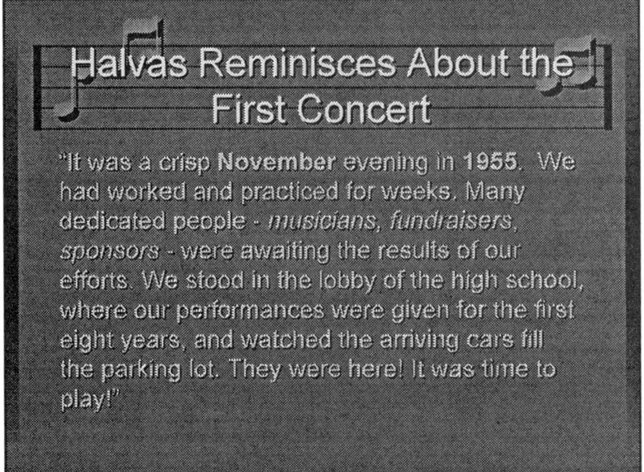

Figure 1 - 13 Completed Slide 4

Figure 1 - 14 Completed Slide 5

1. Start Microsoft Office, if necessary. Use the Microsoft Office toolbar to open *Word.*
2. Open the **history.doc** file from your data disk.
3. Print the document. Read it so that you familiarize yourself with the orchestra's history.

   You will copy the two indented, italicized paragraphs on page 1 to the PowerPoint presentation.
4. Select the first indented paragraph beginning "*The Powell Community Orchestra has...*".
5. Choose **EDIT/Copy** or click on the **COPY** button.
6. Switch to *PowerPoint* using the Microsoft Office toolbar.
7. Open the **history.ppt** presentation.
8. Move to slide 2 ("*The Powell Community Orchestra Mission*").
9. Click in the text block so that the text cursor appears next to the bullet.

CAUTION: *When pasting text into PowerPoint, it is necessary to have a text block or object block selected. You will not be able to edit the text if you paste it directly on a blank slide.*

10. Choose **EDIT/Paste** or click on the **PASTE** button.

    *The selected text from **history.doc** should be pasted into the **history.ppt** presentation. Notice that the color of the text has changed to white, which is the color of all of the body text in this presentation and the font style has been changed from italic to regular.*

PROBLEM SOLVER: *Only the bullet containing the information on the Powell Community Orchestra should appear. If extra blank bullets appear, press the **BACKSPACE** key until they are removed.*

NOTE: *A border will appear around the text when text editing is possible. To make formatting changes to the entire text block you must select the text block so that handles appear around the border. To do this, point to the border and click.*

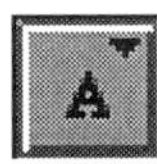

11. Select the text block by clicking on the text border.
12. Decrease the text size by clicking once on the **DECREASE FONT SIZE** button

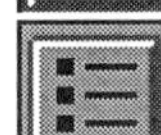

13. Click on the **BULLET ON/OFF** button to erase the bullet.

    Notice that the first line of the paragraph does not line up with the rest of the text. You will use the Ruler to align the text on the left side of the text block.

14. If the Ruler is not showing, choose **VIEW/Ruler**.

    Notice that the ruler looks just like the Word ruler.

15. Place the cursor in the text block.
16. Point to the bottom triangle (Figure 1 - 15) and drag it to the left margin so that it is lined up with the top triangle.

    The text in the text block will now be aligned at the left margin.

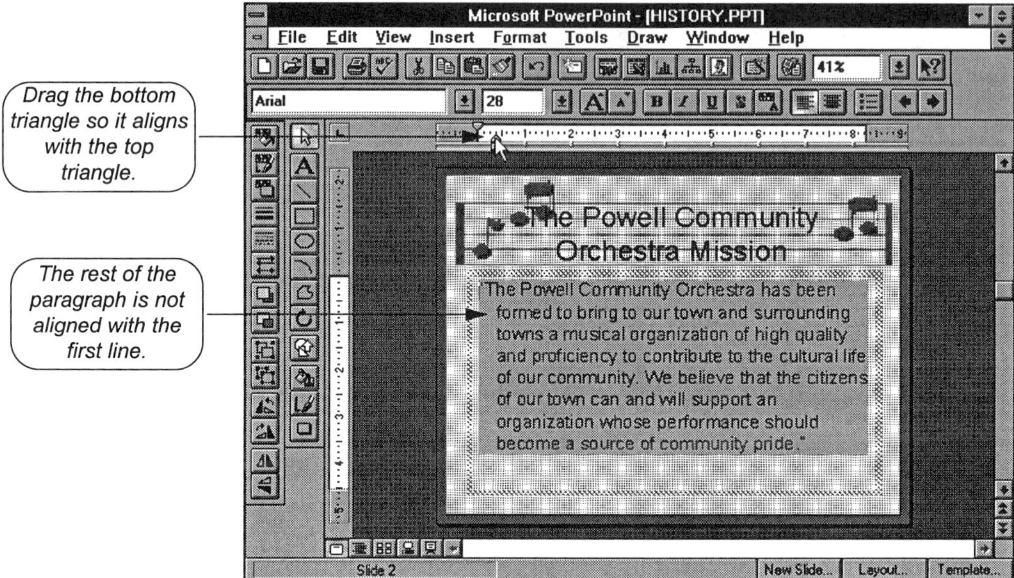

Figure 1 - 15 Using the Ruler to change indents

17. Now make the following changes to the paragraph.
    - Make *Powell Community Orchestra* in the first sentence bold.
    - Italicize *high quality and proficiency* in the first sentence.
18. Use the Microsoft Office toolbar to return to *Word.*
19. Copy the second indented, italicized paragraph, beginning with, "*It was a crisp November evening* ..." and paste it into slide 4 of the **history.ppt** presentation. Refer to steps 4-10 if you need help.
20. Decrease the font size to 28 pt, remove the bullet and align all of the text to the left side of the slide. Refer to steps 11 - 16 if you need help.
21. Now make the following editing changes to the paragraph.
    - Italicize *musicians, fund-raisers*, and *sponsors* in the third sentence.
    - Bold *November* and *1955* in the first sentence.

    Slide 4 should resemble Figure 1 - 13.

22. **Save** the presentation **As: history1.ppt**
23. Print slides 2 and 4 only. Make sure that you mark the **Black & White** check box unless you are using a color printer.
24. Use the Microsoft Office toolbar to switch to *Word.*
25. Close the **history.doc** file without saving the changes.

CAUTION: *Since you are finished working with the Word document, it is a good idea to exit the program. Your machine will have to work harder with more programs open. This will slow the machine down and may cause the system to crash.*

26. Exit from *Word.*
27. Use the Microsoft toolbar to open *Excel.*
28. Open **attend.xls**.

    This worksheet contains attendance figures for the Powell Community Orchestra in five-year blocks since its inception. A bar chart of the attendance figures is also included.
29. Scroll the screen so that you see the entire chart.
30. Select the chart by clicking anywhere in the chart (Figure 1 - 16).

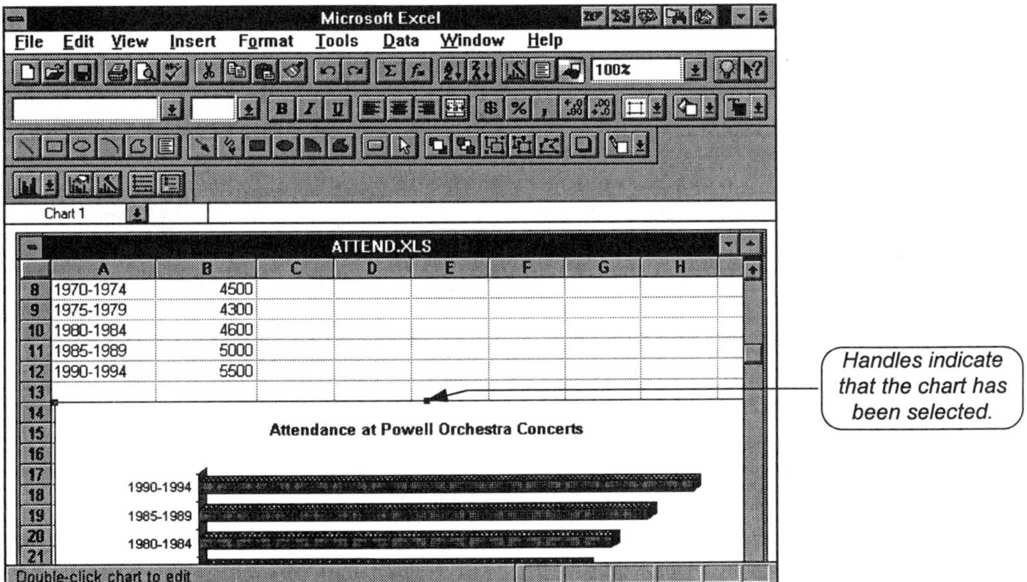

Figure 1 - 16 The selected chart

31. Choose **EDIT/Copy**.
32. Use the Microsoft Office toolbar to switch to *PowerPoint.*
33. Move to slide 5.
34. Choose **EDIT/Paste**.

    The chart is placed in the middle of the slide.
35. Move and size the chart so that it looks like Figure 1 - 14. (**HINT:** Move and size the chart by clicking once to select it. To size, point to one of the handles and drag. To move, point anywhere on the chart *except* the handles, and drag.)
36. You want to increase the font size of the titles on the chart. Try editing the chart by clicking once somewhere in *Attendance at Powell Orchestra Concerts.*

    Nothing happens! The chart cannot be edited using PowerPoint features. Since PowerPoint does not have the features necessary to edit the chart, the chart has been automatically embedded into the document. To edit the chart you would double-click on it and use Excel to edit it. You will learn how to do this in Lesson 2.
37. Save the presentation again using the same name.

38. Print slide 5 using the **Black & White** option.
39. Exit *PowerPoint.*

    You will return to the Excel program.
40. Close **attend.xls** without saving it.
41. Exit *Excel.*

Independent Project 1.3: Copying Data from Excel to Access

So far you have used the three applications in the Standard Version of Microsoft Office to copy and paste. *Microsoft Access*, Office's database package is only included in the Professional Version of Office. Data can also be copied and pasted between *Access* and the other Office applications. This project will give you the opportunity to practice copying worksheet data from *Excel* and pasting it into *Access*. You will also learn to copy data from nonadjacent columns in *Excel* by first hiding the columns that you do not want to copy. This technique also works when copying from *Excel* to *Word* or *PowerPoint*.

In this project you will add data to a database on the paid and volunteer orchestra members for the Powell Orchestra. The orchestra members' names and, if they are paid, their salaries for 1994-95 are part of the **expenses.xls** worksheet. All other information, such as their addresses, telephone numbers, etc., is currently kept only on their written application forms. You have created the database **orchmemb.mdb** and designed two tables, **Professional** and **Volunteer**. Instead of typing all of the data you decide to begin by copying the name, instrument, and, in the case of the professional members, the 1994-1995 salary, from **expenses.xls** and pasting the data into the two **orchmemb.mdb** tables. The commands you use will be identical to those used when copying and pasting from *Excel* to *Word* or *PowerPoint* except that you will use **EDIT/Paste Append** instead of **EDIT/Paste** to insert the data into *Access*. Then you would use the applications filled out by the musicians to add the remaining information about each orchestra member. Figure 1 - 17 shows the completed **Professional** table at the end of the project. Figure 1 - 18 shows a portion of the **Volunteer** table at the end of the project.

1. Open *Excel* and **expenses.xls**.
2. If the **Personnel** sheet is not displayed click on the **Personnel** tab.
3. Print the worksheet.

   There are three sections to the worksheet, one for the conductor, one for the professional musicians and one for the volunteer musicians. First you will copy data on the professional musicians, but you only want to copy the name, position and total compensation. Luckily, there is an easy way to do this. If you copy from Excel to Access, Word, or PowerPoint any columns that you hide will not be copied, so you will first hide the columns you do not want to copy.

   *(If you are copying within Excel, Excel will copy the hidden columns unless you tell it not to. To copy only the visible cells, select the range to be copied and then choose **EDIT/Go To**. In the **Go To** dialog box, click on the **Special** button and mark the **Visible Cells** check box in the **Go To Special** dialog box. Paste the data.)*
4. Select columns **C, D** and **E** by clicking on the column heading of Column **C** and dragging the mouse to the right until columns **C:E** are selected. Make sure the mouse pointer is a ✚.
5. Choose **FORMAT/Column,Hide.**

   *Columns **C, D,** and **E** are no longer visible although a thick black line indicates that some columns are missing.*
6. Select **A9:F26.**

   *Be careful <u>not</u> to select rows **8** or **27**.*

Table: Professional

Name	Position	1994-1995 Salai	Address	City
Erin Antonio	Concert Master	900		
Phyllis Bartholemew	1st Violin	350		
Gladys Boyenga	1st Violin	525		
Elinor Cruz	1st Violin	175		
David Dickie	Princ. 2nd Violin	600		
Robert Finch	2nd Violin	525		
Maude Finley	2nd Violin	525		
Wilbert Harrison	Princ. Viola	600		
Mildred Keith	Viola	175		
John King	Princ. Cello	600		
Eli Kupferberg	Cello	175		
Shawn O'Leary	Princ. Clarinet	600		
Claire Paige	Oboe	525		
Millicent Ringrose	Princ. Bassoon	600		
Carl Rinko	Bassoon	525		
Allen Smith	Timpani	600		
Ruth Winkowsin	Harp	175		
Jessica Poli	Harpsichord	175		
		0		

Figure 1 - 17 The Professional table at the end of the project

Table: Volunteer

Name	Position	1994-1995	Address	City	State	
William Dalton	1st Violin	Yes	50 Grendell Rd.	Powell	CT	0623
Sun-Wong Eisenbe	1st Violin	Yes				
Dudley Farrell	1st Violin	Yes				
Beau Finver	1st Violin	Yes				
Charles Nelson	2nd Violin	Yes				
Prucilla Pinella	2nd Violin	Yes				
John Rice	2nd Violin	Yes				
Pierre Shaughness	2nd Violin	Yes				
Henry Stein	2nd Violin	Yes				
Frederic Thompson	Viola	Yes				
John Verdon	Viola	Yes				
Stanley Zebrowski	Viola	Yes				
Joel Albert	Viola	Yes				
Allan Berry	Cello	Yes				
Karin Bliss	Cello	Yes				
Bob Cartwright	Cello	Yes				
Martin Composto	Cello	Yes				
Gertie Delubert	Bass	Yes				
Doris Dodd	Bass	Yes				
Simon McLantern	Bass	Yes				
Hugo Mikulewicz	Clarinet	Yes				
Jody Newt	Flute	Yes				
Michelle Scherb	Flute	Yes				

Figure 1 - 18 The Volunteer table at the end of the project

7. Copy the selected range.
8. Open *Access*.
9. In *Access* open the database **orchmemb.mdb**.
10. Open the **Professional** table.

    The database contains no records. Maximize the table. The database includes the fields: Name, Position, 1994-1995 Comp., Address, City, State and Zip. Scroll the screen if necessary to see all fields. Scroll back so that the Name field is visible on the screen.

11. The insertion point should be in the **Name** field of record **1**. If it isn't, click in the **Name** field.
12. Click on **EDIT/Paste Append** to paste the data copied from *Access*.

    Paste Append *is used because you want to add the data to the end of the database as new records.* ***Paste*** *would insert the data in the selected cell(s) rather than create 18 new records and is best used to insert data into a single field.*

    Because database changes save as soon as you leave the current record, Access displays an alert box making sure that you want to save the changes (Figure 1 - 19).

Microsoft Access

You've just pasted 18 record(s). Choose OK to save your changes or Cancel to undo your changes.

OK Cancel Help

Figure 1 - 19 Access' warning that the new records will be saved with the database

CAUTION: *We designed our database table so that the fields were in the same order as the worksheet columns. If this is not the case, you must re-order the fields so that they match the columns in the worksheet (or Word table) from which you are copying. You can move the fields back to their original location after you paste the new data. Access will usually supply error messages if there is a mismatch between the records you are pasting and the fields into which you want them pasted. For example, if the data you copy is too wide to fit in the database fields, it will either be truncated or the records will be added to a separate error table. If the data does not match the data type, Access will display an error message and will not create the new records.*

13. Check that the alert box matches Figure 1 - 19 and click on **OK** if it does. If it contains different information, choose **Cancel** and repeat this project from step 2.

    The name, position and 1994-1995 Comp for the 18 paid orchestra members should be inserted into the Professional table.

PROBLEM SOLVER: *If the data was not placed in the first record, delete any blank records at the beginning of the table.*

14. Close the **Professional** table.
15. Open the **Volunteer** table.

    *A blank record appears on the screen. The **Yes/No** field contains the entry "Yes" because when we designed the table we instructed Access to automatically enter "Yes" in this field for new records. Next year if you added new volunteers who did not perform in the 1994-1995 season, you would either replace each Yes entry with No or change the Default Value in the design table.*

16. Switch back to *Excel*.
17. To display the hidden columns, select columns **B:F** and the choose **FORMAT/Column,Unhide**.
18. Copy the data on the volunteer musicians from cells **A31:B60.** Use **EDIT/Paste Append** to insert the data into the **Volunteer** table in **orchmemb.mdb**.

    *This time you should have inserted **30** records. The **1994-1995** field is a **Yes/No** field. Access has entered **Yes** for all of the record.*

19. Here's the data from William Dalton's application form. Add it to his record:

Address	**50 Grendell Rd.**
City	**Powell**
State	**CT**
Zip	**06231**

Since this is not a data entry exercise, we will end this project before you enter the rest of the data. However, you can see how much data entry time was saved by copying the data from *Excel*.

20. Use the **PRINT** button to print the **Professional** and **Volunteer** tables.
21. Close the table and database and exit from *Access*.
22. Close the **expenses.xls** worksheet *without* saving changes. Exit from *Excel*.

ALTERNATE METHOD: *The procedures used in this project can also be used to copy data from a Word table and paste it into Access or to copy part or all of an Access table into a Word table. Alternatively, the* ***INSERT/Database*** *command in Word can be used to copy data from Access and paste into a Word table. This command gives you the opportunity to copy all or part of a table or an existing query. Copy and paste can also be used to bring data from Access into Excel.*

Lesson

Embedding Objects

Objectives

In this lesson you will learn how to:

- Understand the advantages and disadvantages of object embedding
- Copy worksheet data from *Excel* and embed it into *Word*
- Edit an *Excel* worksheet object embedded in *Word*
- Embed a new *Excel* worksheet object into a *Word* document
- Change the amount of an embedded worksheet that is displayed in a *Word* document
- Embed an existing *Excel* chart into a *Word* document
- Embed a *Word* table into a *PowerPoint* presentation
- Embed a new *Word* document into an *Excel* worksheet

THE TWO USES OF EMBEDDING

Unlike pasting, or linking, embedding can be used in two very different ways. The first, embedding *existing* data into another document, will be the focus of the first project in this lesson. An embedded object becomes part of the document in which it is embedded, but unlike pasted data it only can be edited using the commands of the application that created it rather than the commands of the application in which it is contained.

In the second use, embedding is used to create *new* data using the tools of an application that is different from the one that will contain the data. This second use of embedding is an excellent example of Microsoft Office's switch in emphasis from the *application* that you are working *in* to the *task* that you are working *on*. When you *embed a new object*, you are simply using the application that best handles the task that you want to perform. The data remains in the destination or "container" application and the commands of the application you are using to create the document are at your disposal without you having to leave the destination application. If you have completed *Getting Started with Microsoft PowerPoint 4.0 for Windows,* you have already practiced embedding new objects into existing documents. Instead of including its own commands for creating tables, worksheets or charts, *PowerPoint* allows the use of *Word, Excel,* and *Microsoft Graph* commands to embed new *Word* tables, *Excel* worksheets, and *Microsoft Graph* charts into a presentation. In the second project in this lesson you will embed a new *Excel* worksheet into a W*ord* document.

PROJECT 1 DESCRIPTION

As in Lesson 1, you once again want to include part of an *Excel* worksheet in your *Word* document. The orchestra receives an annual grant from the Community Orchestra Fund. Since the goal of the Community Orchestra Fund is to promote opportunities for volunteer musicians to perform before an audience, you must prove that a majority of the participants in each concert were unpaid. Part of your expenses worksheet (**expenses.xls**) includes fees for the paid musicians. You must include this data in your report to the Fund. However, you also need to perform some new calculations on the copied data. Therefore, you want to be able to access *Excel* to perform these calculations after the data has been inserted into *Word*. To be able to do this, instead of copying and pasting the worksheet data, you will copy and embed the data. The file **orchfund.doc** contains the beginning of your letter to the Community Orchestra Fund. When completed your letter will resemble Figure 2 - 1.

Anthony Souza
Director
Community Orchestra Fund
555 Main Street
Powell, NY 10555

Dear Mr. Souza:

The Powell Community Orchestra has just completed another successful year. Your continued support has contributed to our success. We feel that we have continued to maintain an orchestra of the highest quality while providing abundant opportunity for volunteer musicians to perform in their community.

As required by your grant I have included a list of orchestra personnel for all of our concerts and the amount that each person was paid. As you can see more than half of the musicians were volunteers.

Name	Position	Concert 1	Concert 2	Concert 3
Erin Antonio	Concert Master	300	300	300
Phyllis Bartholemew	1st Violin	175		175
Gladys Boyenga	1st Violin	175	175	175
Elinor Cruz	1st Violin		175	
David Dickie	Princ. 2nd Violin	200	200	200
Robert Finch	2nd Violin	175	175	175
Maude Finley	2nd Violin	175	175	175
Wilbert Harrison	Princ. Viola	200	200	200
Mildred Keith	Viola		175	
John King	Princ. Cello	200	200	200
Eli Kupferberg	Cello	175		
Shawn O'Leary	Princ. Clarinet	200	200	200
Claire Paige	Oboe	175	175	175
Millicent Ringrose	Princ. Bassoon	200	200	200
Carl Rinko	Bassoon	175	175	175
Allen Smith	Timpani	200	200	200
Ruth Winkowsin	Harp		175	
Jessica Poli	Harpsichord			175

The list of volunteer orchestra members for each concert follows.

Name	Position	Concert 1	Concert 2	Concert 3
William Dalton	1st Violin	x	x	
Sun-Wong Eisenberg	1st Violin	x		x
Dudley Farrell	1st Violin	x	x	x
Beau Finver	1st Violin		x	x
Charles Nelson	2nd Violin	x	x	
Prucilla Pinella	2nd Violin	x		x
John Rice	2nd Violin	x	x	
Pierre Shaughnessy	2nd Violin			x
Henry Stein	2nd Violin		x	x
Frederic Thompson	Viola	x	x	x
John Verdon	Viola	x	x	
Stanley Zebrowski	Viola	x		x
Joel Albert	Viola			x
Allan Berry	Cello	x	x	x
Karin Bliss	Cello	x	x	x
Bob Cartwright	Cello			x
Martin Composto	Cello	x	x	
Gertie Delubert	Bass	x	x	
Doris Dodd	Bass	x		x
Simon McLantern	Bass		x	x
Hugo Mikulewicz	Clarinet	x	x	x
Jody Newt	Flute	x	x	
Michelle Scherb	Flute		x	x
Thomas Vinci	Oboe	x	x	x
George Wagner	Bassoon		x	x
Carmen Zazula	French Horn	x		
Harris Louton	French Horn		x	x
John Peter	Trumpet		x	
Reni Gertner	Trumpet		x	
Susan Knowles	Percussion	x	x	
	Total Volunteers	19	22	19
	Total Paid	14	15	14
	Total Orchestra	33	37	33
	% Volunteers	58%	59%	58%

As you can see we have used a number of different volunteers and the orchestra for each concert has included more than 55% volunteer members.

We are very pleased with both the quality of our concerts and community involvement. Enclosed is our completed application for next year's funding. We hope that we can count on your continued support.

Sincerely,

Jessica Stand

Figure 2 - 1 The completed document

EMBEDDING AN OBJECT

When you embed an object created in one application into another application, you retain a connection between the embedded object and the application in which it was created. This connection allows you to use the tools and commands of the source application to edit the data in the destination document. However, there is no connection between the embedded object and the source data, so changes made to the source data after the embedding has been done are *not* made to the embedded (destination) object. As with copying and pasting, if you change the original data and you want these same revisions in the embedded object, you must re-embed the (revised) data or make the same changes to it that you made to the original data. You may also keep the source and destination objects alike by linking them. You will learn about linking objects in Lesson 3.

Embedding Part of expenses.xls in orchfund.doc

As we did in Lesson 1, let's see which method you should use to include the data from **expenses.xls** in **orchfund.doc**. The questions that we asked and the answers for this project follow.

- Do I expect the source data to change? If it changes, do I want the data in the destination document to change also?

  The answer to this question is very much the same as it was in Lesson 1. The data in the part of the worksheet that you will copy is not expected to change as the concerts are over and all of the orchestra members have been paid. Furthermore, you want to make changes to the data in the worksheet that need not be made to the original worksheet. If you linked the source and destination data, any changes made would appear in both locations, so you do not want to link the source and destination documents.

- Will I need to edit the data once it is in the destination document? If so, do I want to use the source application or the destination application to do the editing?

  The answer to this question is different from the one we made in Lesson 1. In Lesson 1 we wanted to use the formatting commands of Word to edit the worksheet data. In this project our editing changes require us to make some calculations, which are best made in Excel. Therefore, we want to use the source application, Excel, to edit the data.

  If the answer to this question is that you want to use the source application for editing you must ask one more question.

- If I want to use the source application for the editing, is it available on the computer that will be used to edit the destination document?

  The computer that you are using for this project must have both Word and Excel on it, so the program you need to edit the data (Excel) is on your computer. These answers meet the criteria for embedding an object.

Use embedding to share data if:

- The embedded data in the document does *not* need to change if the original data in the source document changes.
- You want to make changes to the embedded data that can best be made using the commands of the source application.
- The source application is on the computer that you will be using to edit the destination document.

EMBEDDING AN EXISTING OBJECT

The procedure for embedding part of one document into another is almost identical to that for pasting a copied object — with one important difference. To embed data, you will begin by copying the data as you did in Lesson 1. However, after you switch to the destination document, you will use the **Paste Special** command from the **EDIT** menu instead of **Paste** to insert the data from the clipboard into the destination document. Therefore, you must use the menu, not the toolbar button to insert the copied data. You must also make sure that the data is pasted as an object of the appropriate type, rather than as formatted or unformatted text.

To embed data from one application into another:

- Select the data in the source application.
- Choose **EDIT/Copy** or click on the **COPY** toolbar button .
- Activate the destination application by clicking on its button on the Office toolbar.
- Open the destination document, if necessary, and move the insertion point to the place at which the data should be pasted.
- Choose **EDIT/Paste Special.**
- In the **Paste Special** dialog box:
    - Choose the **PASTE** option button, if it is not already chosen.
    - In the **As** list box, choose the listing that describes the type of object that you are embedding (i.e., in this project, *Microsoft Excel 5.0 Worksheet Object*). Do *not* leave the choice as *Formatted Text (RFT)* or you will be pasting rather than embedding the object.
    - Click on **OK**.

NOTE: *Embedded data must fit on one page in Word. Therefore, if the object is too long to fit on the current page, it will be placed on the next page. If the worksheet range is too big to fit on an entire page, Word will automatically decrease the font of the embedded worksheet to fit as much as it can and then display only as much of the object as can be shown on one page. To include a Long Excel range in Word, you must paste rather than embed the range.*

CAUTION: *Even though only the part of the worksheet (or other object) that you copied will appear in the destination document, a copy of the entire source file is embedded in the destination file. This takes up a lot of storage space on the disk, but is otherwise not a problem if the person embedding the object is the only one who will have access to the destination file. However, if someone else is going to have access to the destination file, make sure that there is nothing anywhere in the source file that other people should not see. For example, in this project, you will copy only part of one sheet of the Excel workbook into Word. However, another sheet in the source workbook contains data on other orchestra expenses. This information will be available to anyone who has a copy of the file with the embedded worksheet. So, you need to be careful about who has a copy of your destination document.*

Activity 2.1: Embedding an Excel Worksheet Range into Word

In this activity you will open **orchfund.doc**, the file that contains the beginning of the letter to the Community Orchestra Fund, and **expenses.xls**, which contains the budget data which needs to be included in the letter. You will then copy the data from **expenses.xls** and embed it in **orchfund.doc**.

1. Start *Microsoft Office*, if necessary. Use the Office toolbar to open *Word.*
2. Open the file **orchfund.doc**, which is on your data disk.

***Orchfund.doc** is the beginning of a letter to the Community Orchestra Fund documenting the Powell Community Orchestra's compliance with the Fund's rules requiring use of a majority of volunteer musicians in the orchestra concerts.*

3. Print the letter. Read it so that you will understand how the worksheet data will fit.
4. Move the insertion point to the end of the document.

   The insertion point should be on a blank line two lines below the last paragraph. You are now ready to include the data from your worksheet.
5. Switch to *Excel* and open the file **expenses.xls**.
6. Click on the **Personnel** tab at the bottom of the worksheet to display the sheet listing the musicians for all three concerts, the salaries paid to the professional musicians, and the concerts in which the volunteers played.

   If you completed Independent Project 1.3 you have already used this worksheet.
7. Print the worksheet.

   Notice that the worksheet is longer than one page. There are three sections to the worksheet, one for the conductor, one for the professional musicians, and one for the volunteer musicians. First, you will copy the data on the professional musicians.
8. Select cells **A8:E26** (do *not* include the totals in row **27** or column **F**).

   Figure 2 - 2 shows the selected range.
9. Choose **EDIT/Copy** or click on the **COPY** toolbar button.

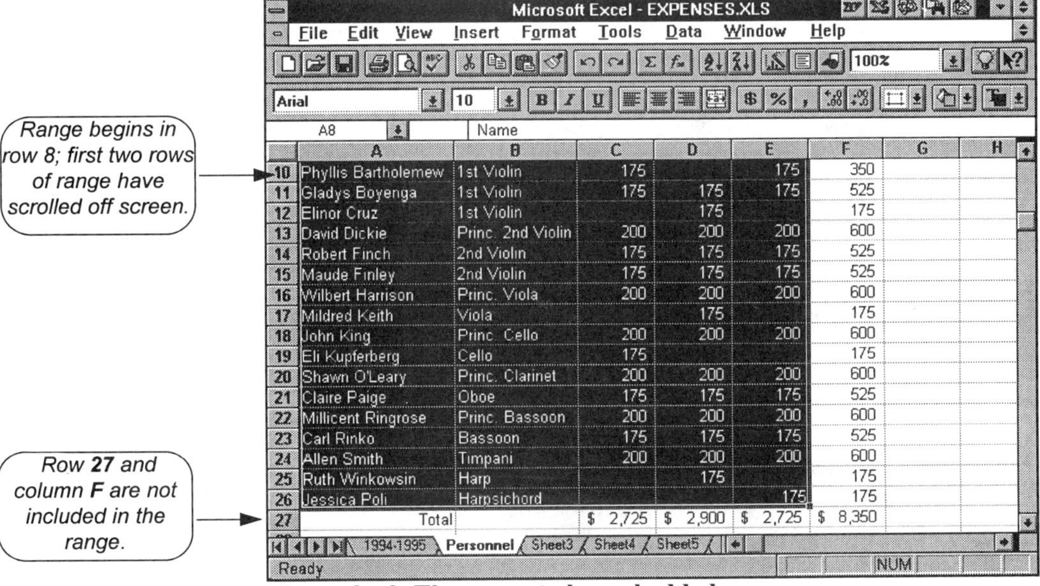

	A	B	C	D	E	F
10	Phyllis Bartholemew	1st Violin	175		175	350
11	Gladys Boyenga	1st Violin	175	175	175	525
12	Elinor Cruz	1st Violin		175		175
13	David Dickie	Princ. 2nd Violin	200	200	200	600
14	Robert Finch	2nd Violin	175	175	175	525
15	Maude Finley	2nd Violin	175	175	175	525
16	Wilbert Harrison	Princ. Viola	200	200	200	600
17	Mildred Keith	Viola		175		175
18	John King	Princ. Cello	200	200	200	600
19	Eli Kupferberg	Cello	175			175
20	Shawn O'Leary	Princ. Clarinet	200	200	200	600
21	Claire Paige	Oboe	175	175	175	525
22	Millicent Ringrose	Princ. Bassoon	200	200	200	600
23	Carl Rinko	Bassoon	175	175	175	525
24	Allen Smith	Timpani	200	200	200	600
25	Ruth Winkowsin	Harp		175		175
26	Jessica Poli	Harpsichord			175	175
27	Total		$ 2,725	$ 2,900	$ 2,725	$ 8,350

Figure 2 - 2 The range to be embedded

10. Switch back to *Word*.

    The insertion point should be at the end of the document.
11. Choose **EDIT/Paste Special**.

    *The **Paste Special** dialog box will appear. The **PASTE** option button should be selected. In the **As** list box, **Formatted Text (RFT)** will also be selected (Figure 2 - 3).*

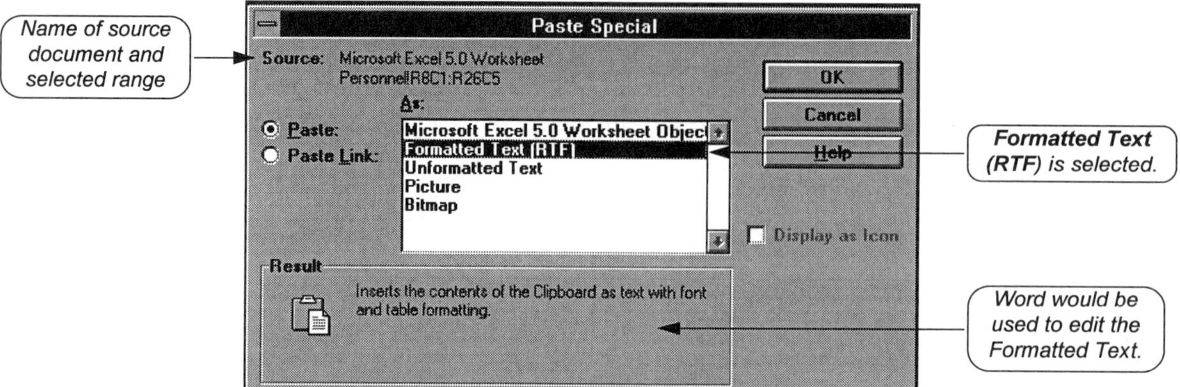

Figure 2 - 3 The Paste Special dialog box as it first appears

NOTE: *When **EDIT/Paste Special** is chosen, the contents of the **Paste Special** dialog box indicate how the contents of the clipboard would be inserted into the document if the **EDIT/Paste** command were chosen. **Paste Special** then gives you the option of changing these selections so that the object can be embedded or linked. Read the **Result** portion of the dialog box. It indicates that if you pressed **ENTER** now the copied portion of the Excel worksheet would be inserted as text with font and table formatting. You already know this from Lesson 1 where the pasted Excel worksheet was inserted into Word as a Word table with its font, alignment in the table, etc., similar to what it had been in Excel.*

12. Click on **Microsoft Excel 5.0 Worksheet Object** in the **As** list box.

    *Look at the **Result** portion of the dialog box now (Figure 2 - 4). It indicates that the copied portion of the Excel worksheet will be inserted as an object which can be edited in Excel as an Excel worksheet. This is the definition of an **embedded** object, so you have made the correct choice.*

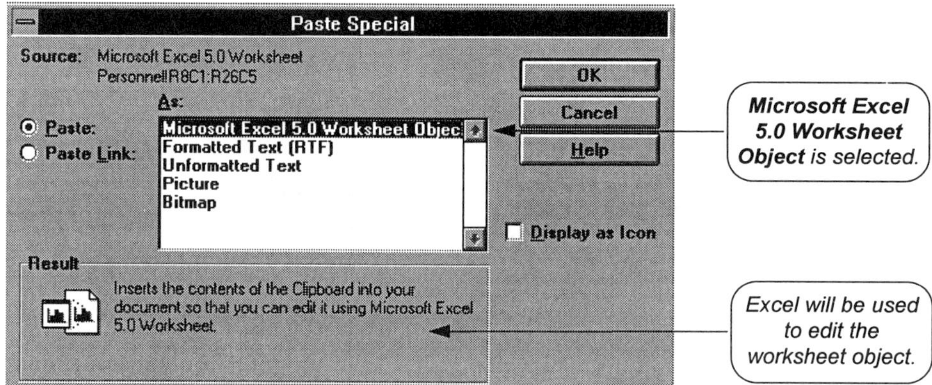

Figure 2 - 4 The Paste Special dialog box changed so that copied data will be embedded

NOTE: *There are three other formats in which the clipboard contents can be inserted into the Word document. **Unformatted Text** inserts the Clipboard contents as text without any formatting. If you used this to insert an Excel worksheet, it would appear as several lines of text rather than as a table. **Picture** and **bitmap** insert the contents of the Clipboard as two different types of pictures. Both are edited using graphics tools; there is no necessary connection between the picture or bitmap and the application in which the object was created.*

13. Click on **OK** or press **ENTER** to embed the worksheet.

    Don't worry if the worksheet does not appear immediately (even after the dialog box disappears it takes a while for the worksheet range to appear in your letter); the time lapse can be substantial depending on the speed of your computer. Since the object is going to be edited by the application in which it was created, it is should appear as it appears in the original application. For example, unlike the pasted worksheet range in Lesson 1, the full gridlines from the Excel worksheet appear on the screen and will be printed.

14. Click *once* anywhere in the embedded worksheet.

    Handles appear around the embedded worksheet range (Figure 2 - 5). The Word insertion point does not appear in the embedded worksheet because you cannot edit the data using Word commands. As the status bar indicates, Word considers this portion of your document to be a Microsoft Excel 5.0 worksheet and you must "Double-click to Edit Microsoft Excel 5.0 Worksheet."

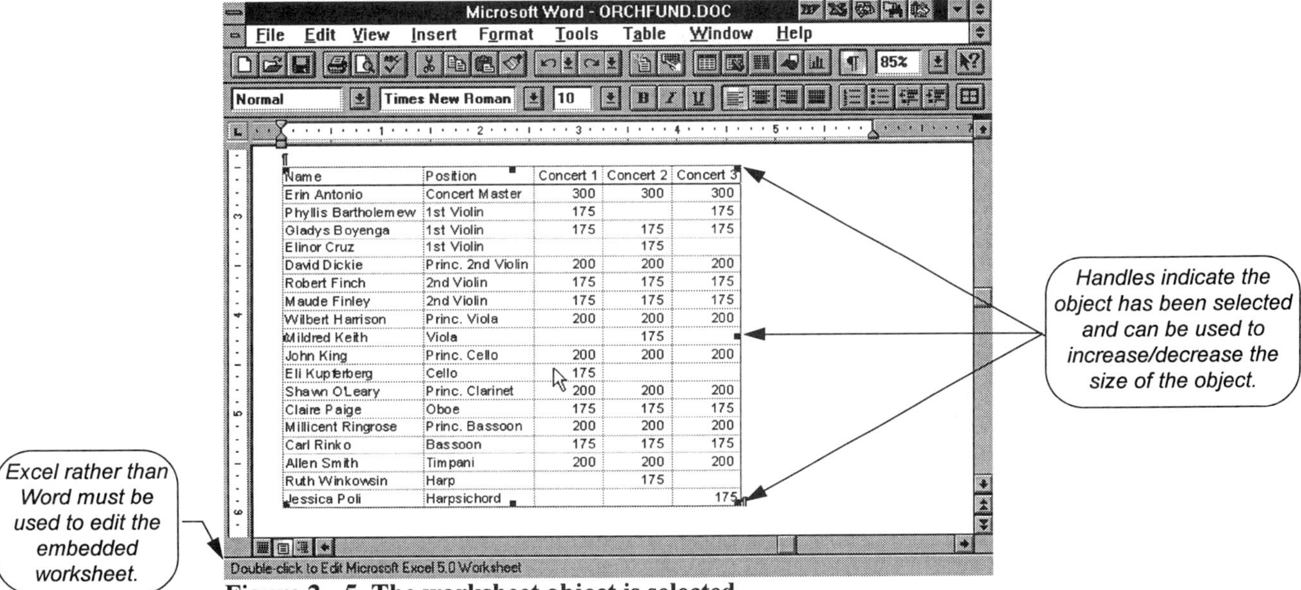

Name	Position	Concert 1	Concert 2	Concert 3
Erin Antonio	Concert Master	300	300	300
Phyllis Bartholemew	1st Violin	175		175
Gladys Boyenga	1st Violin	175	175	175
Elinor Cruz	1st Violin		175	
David Dickie	Princ. 2nd Violin	200	200	200
Robert Finch	2nd Violin	175	175	175
Maude Finley	2nd Violin	175	175	175
Wilbert Harrison	Princ. Viola	200	200	200
Mildred Keith	Viola		175	
John King	Princ. Cello	200	200	200
Eli Kupferberg	Cello	175		
Shawn O'Leary	Princ. Clarinet	200	200	200
Claire Paige	Oboe	175	175	175
Millicent Ringrose	Princ. Bassoon	200	200	200
Carl Rinko	Bassoon	175	175	175
Allen Smith	Timpani	200	200	200
Ruth Winkowsin	Harp		175	
Jessica Poli	Harpsichord			175

Figure 2 - 5 The worksheet object is selected

CAUTION: *As the handles indicate, the embedded Excel worksheet has been selected. Therefore, if you press the* **DEL** *key, Word will delete the embedded object. Or, if you type text, and the* **Typing Replaces Selection** *option has been turned on, Word will think you want to replace the embedded worksheet with the new text you type! So, be careful what you do while an embedded document is selected.*

NOTE: *If you completed Lesson 6 in Getting Started with Microsoft Excel 5.0 for Windows, you created a chart on the existing worksheet. Another way of describing this is that you embedded the chart on the worksheet. When you clicked once on the chart, you selected it and could only move or resize it. To edit it, you had to click twice.*

The same procedures apply to other embedded objects. When the embedded object is clicked on once, it is selected (as indicated by the handles on the frame), and can only be moved, resized or have formats (such as Borders) applied to the entire object. To move the object, click anywhere within it and drag it to the desired location. To resize the object, click on one of the handles. When the mouse pointer changes to a ↔ drag the mouse to increase or decrease the size of the object. If a selected Excel worksheet object is resized, the size of the font is increased or decreased so that it takes up the new object size; the amount of data displayed is not changed. Resizing other types of objects may cause distortion.

15. Click anywhere outside of the embedded table to deselect it.
16. Press **CTRL+END** if necessary to position the cursor at the end of the document.
17. Press **ENTER** twice.
18. Type the following paragraph:

    The list of volunteer orchestra members for each concert follows.
19. Press **ENTER** twice.
20. Switch to *Excel.*
21. Select cells **A30:E64. This range includes four blank rows at the end of the list of volunteer orchestra members. Be sure that your range goes down to row 64 or you will have trouble with later portions of this activity.**

    You have included four blank rows at the end of the worksheet range because you are going to add some calculations to the end of the embedded worksheet. It is possible to extend the displayed range of a worksheet after it is embedded, but it is easier to include the extra cells in the range before embedding it, so that is what you have done here. In Project 2 in this lesson you will learn to change the amount of the embedded worksheet displayed in the Word document.
22. Use **Copy** and **Paste Special** to embed the newly selected range into **orchfund.doc**. (Refer to steps 9 through 13 if you need help.) Remember to change the object type to **Excel 5.0 Worksheet Object.**

    Your worksheet will appear on page 2 of ***orchfund.doc*** *because the entire worksheet range cannot fit on page 1 and Word will not split an embedded object over two pages. This limits the length of embedded worksheets (or other objects) to one page, although as explained before the size of the original object may shrink to fit more of it on one page.*
23. To test that you embedded the worksheet correctly, scroll down the screen so that you can see the end of the worksheet and make sure that four blank lines are included at the bottom (Figure 2 - 6). Then click anywhere in the worksheet and check that the worksheet is surrounded by handles and that the message *Double-click to Edit Microsoft Excel 5.0 Worksheet* appears on the status bar.

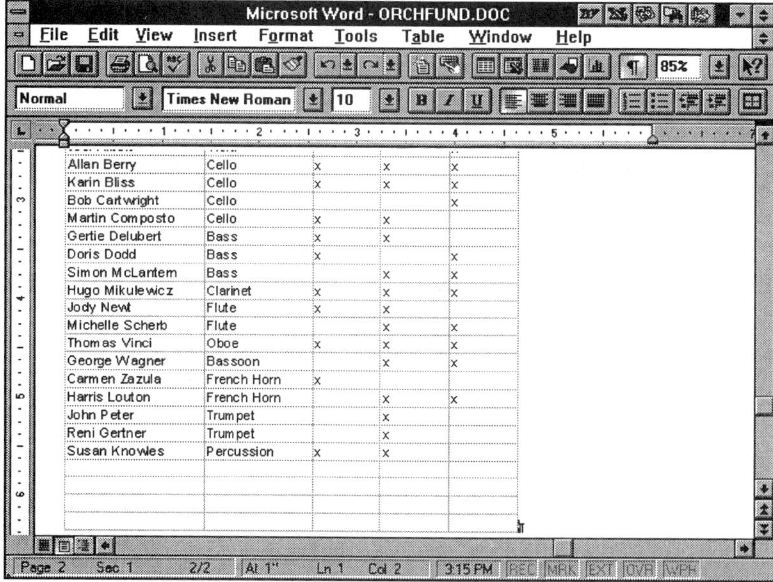

Figure 2 - 6 The embedded worksheet with four blank lines

PROBLEM SOLVER: *If you have not embedded the worksheet correctly, click on the* ***UNDO*** *button on the Standard toolbar or choose* ***EDIT/Undo (Paste Special)****. Follow the instructions in steps 21 and 22 again.*

24. Click outside of the worksheet to deselect it.
25. **Save** your document **as: fundltr.doc**
26. Although you actually use *Excel* to edit your document, you do not need to start *Excel*. The embedded *Excel* object contains all of the information necessary to give you access to *Excel*'s commands. To see this more clearly, switch back to *Excel* and **exit** from *Excel.* If you are asked if you want to *Save changes in 'EXPENSES.XLS'?,* choose **No**.
27. If an alert box asking *Save large Clipboard from '[EXPENSES.XLS]Personnel'?* appears, choose **No**.

    Since the selection copied from Excel is large and will remain on the clipboard until you cut or paste something else, you will probably be asked if you want to save the large clipboard. Saving the clipboard does not mean saving its contents in a file. It means that the contents will remain on the clipboard even when the application is closed. The advantage of saving the clipboard is that you can paste the data somewhere else. The disadvantage is that you are taking up memory. Therefore, you should choose ***NO*** *so that you will have as many resources as possible to do the other activities in this lesson.*

EDITING AN EMBEDDED WORKSHEET IN A WORD DOCUMENT

One of the advantages of object embedding is that you can use the full commands of the source application to make changes in the embedded object without leaving the file in which it is embedded. There are several different ways to initiate editing an embedded object. They all use the source application, but the appearance of your screen may differ during editing.

To edit an embedded object:

- Open the embedded object by:
    - Double-clicking on the embedded object or clicking on the embedded object once and choosing **EDIT/Spreadsheet Object*** **, Edit**

      If you are editing an Excel worksheet (or spreadsheet) object in Word, a small Excel application window will appear <u>*within*</u> *the Word window. The title bar will continue to say Microsoft Word and the name of the Word document, but the menus and toolbars will change to Excel's, and an Excel formula bar will be added. The embedded Excel worksheet will be in a separate window within the Word document window and it will contain the Excel row and column labels and scroll bars. In other situations, double-clicking or choosing* ***EDIT/[Object], Edit*** *may open the embedded object in a full-sized source application window separate from the destination application window.*
    - Or selecting the embedded object by clicking on it *once*, and then choosing **EDIT/Spreadsheet Object*,Open.**

      When this command is chosen, the worksheet (or other embedded) object will open in a full-sized source application window separate from the destination application.
- Edit the embedded object using the editing and formatting techniques of the source application (in this case, *Excel*).

---

* If the embedded object is not a worksheet, the name of that object (Chart Object, PowerPoint Object, etc.) will be substituted for Spreadsheet Object on the Edit menu. Also note that *Word* sometimes refers to *Excel* worksheet data as a Worksheet Object and sometimes as a Spreadsheet Object!

- End editing by:
  - Pressing **ESC** twice (in some situations, pressing once is enough) or clicking in the destination document window outside of the embedded object twice. These techniques work if the embedded object is in a small window within the destination document (as it will be when you edit an embedded worksheet by double-clicking on it).
  - Or if you are editing the embedded object in its own full-sized window, choosing **FILE/Update** and then choosing **FILE/Close** to close the document and return to the source application or **FILE/Exit** to close the application and return to the destination document. If the command **FILE/Exit and Return To (the destination application)** or **FILE/Close and Return to (the destination application)** appears on the **File** menu, use that command instead.

Activity 2.2: Editing an Embedded Worksheet in Word

In this activity you will make two sets of changes to the worksheets that you embedded in your letter. First, you decide that you want to make the column headings (Name, Position, etc.) in both embedded worksheets bold. Second, although the embedded worksheets provide the Community Orchestra Fund with the raw data about who played in the Powell Community Orchestra concerts, they contain no summary statistics. Therefore, you want to add some calculations to the second embedded worksheet which indicate how many members were paid and how many were volunteer.

1. Switch to **fundltr.doc** if it is not already on the screen.
2. Maximize both **fundltr.doc** and *Word*, if they are not already maximized.
3. Press **CTRL+HOME** and then scroll down the screen so that the entire first worksheet is visible on the screen. Make sure that at least two lines above the top of the worksheet are visible (Figure 2 - 7) so that you will be able to see the full *Excel* window.

PROBLEM SOLVER: *If toolbars in addition to the formatting and standard toolbars are visible there will not be enough room. Choose **VIEW/Toolbars** and remove the marks from all of the check boxes except **Formatting** and **Standard**. You may also use the **View** menu to remove the ruler from the screen.*

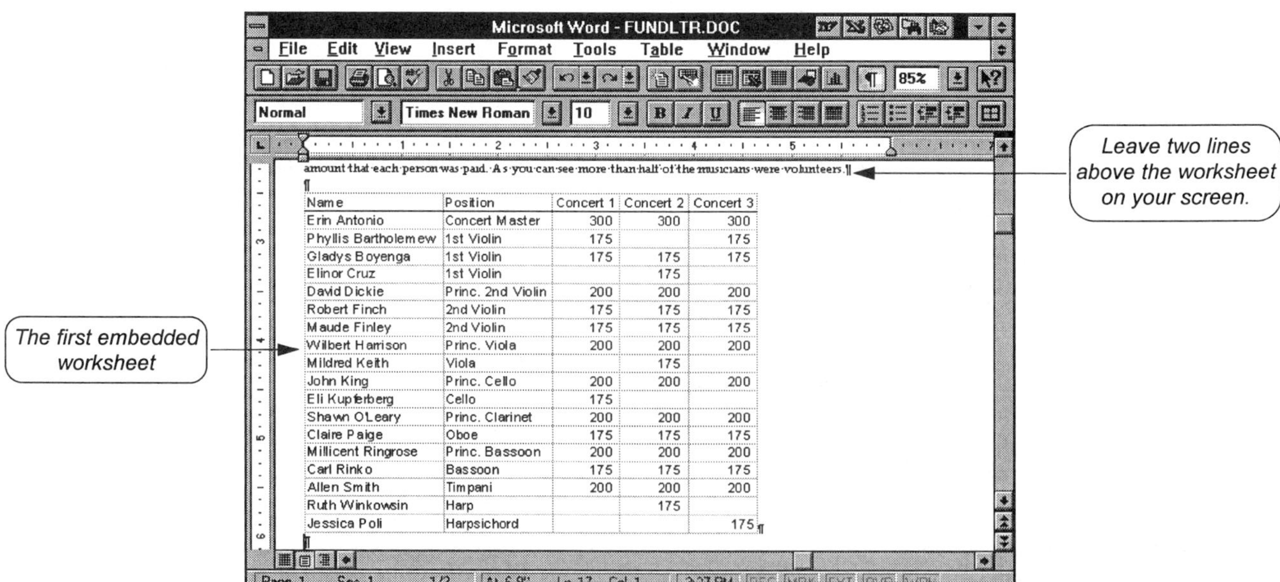

Name	Position	Concert 1	Concert 2	Concert 3
Erin Antonio	Concert Master	300	300	300
Phyllis Bartholemew	1st Violin	175		175
Gladys Boyenga	1st Violin	175	175	175
Elinor Cruz	1st Violin		175	
David Dickie	Princ. 2nd Violin	200	200	200
Robert Finch	2nd Violin	175	175	175
Maude Finley	2nd Violin	175	175	175
Wilbert Harrison	Princ. Viola	200	200	200
Mildred Keith	Viola		175	
John King	Princ. Cello	200	200	200
Eli Kupferberg	Cello	175		
Shawn O'Leary	Princ. Clarinet	200	200	200
Claire Paige	Oboe	175	175	175
Millicent Ringrose	Princ. Bassoon	200	200	200
Carl Rinko	Bassoon	175	175	175
Allen Smith	Timpani	200	200	200
Ruth Winkowsin	Harp		175	
Jessica Poli	Harpsichord			175

Figure 2 - 7 The entire embedded worksheet is visible

4. Double-click anywhere in the embedded worksheet.

   A small Excel window should (eventually) appear within the Word document (Figure 2 - 8). The Word title bar, scroll bars, and status bar should remain on the screen. Look carefully at the menus and toolbar. The ***Data*** *menu is present; this is an Excel menu, not a Word menu. The other menu names are the same in Word and Excel, but if you opened any of the menus they would contain the Excel commands. Similarly, the toolbars are those of Excel (see the* ***AUTOSUM*** *and* ***FUNCTION WIZARD*** *buttons). The worksheet appears inside the small Excel window which includes the Excel scroll bars, column headers (A, B, etc.) and row headers (8, 9, 10, etc.)*

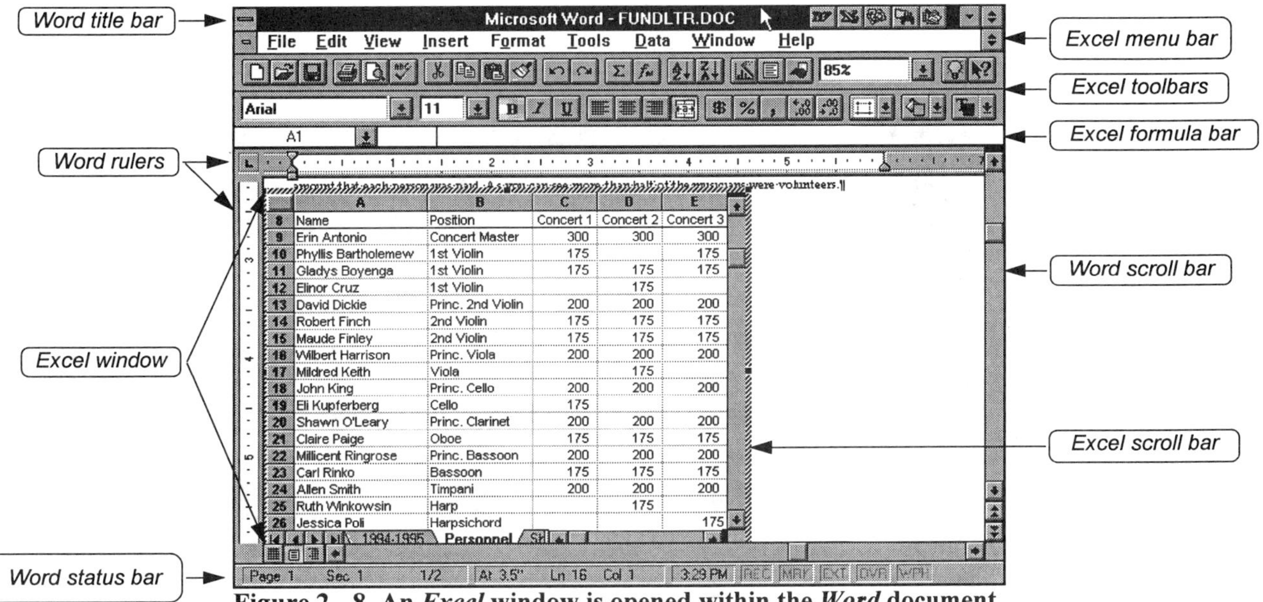

Figure 2 - 8 An *Excel* window is opened within the *Word* document window

5. Select **A8:E8**.

CAUTION: *Be careful not to scroll the worksheet window. If you are editing an embedded worksheet in a small window within the Word document, the part of the worksheet that is visible in the Excel window when you return to Word will be embedded in the Word document even if this was not the part of the worksheet that you originally embedded. Therefore, if you have accidentally scrolled the document, make sure that you scroll it back so that row* ***8*** *is the first row in the window before you complete step 7 in these instructions.*

6. Use the menus or toolbar to **bold** the column headings (Figure 2 - 9).

7. When you are done, press **ESC** twice or click twice on any part of the *Word* document outside of the *Excel* window.

PROBLEM SOLVER: *If the column headings, name, position, etc., are not the top line of your embedded worksheet, double-click on the worksheet. Scroll the worksheet so that the column headings are on the first line visible in the worksheet window. Press* ***ESC*** *twice to close the Excel window.*

8. Scroll down to page 2 so that you can see part of the second embedded worksheet.

   This worksheet is too big to fit on one screen on most monitors (Figure 2 - 10). When editing an embedded worksheet that is too big to fit on the screen, it is better to edit it in a larger separate screen. Otherwise, it can be difficult to move to all parts of the worksheet.

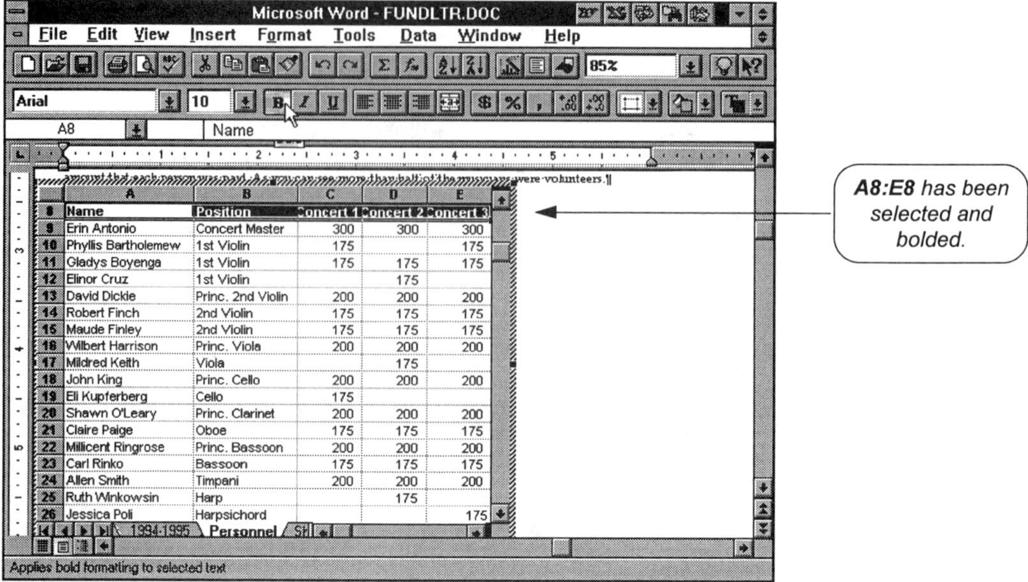

Figure 2 - 9 Click on the BOLD button to bold the column headings

PROBLEM SOLVER: *If your embedded worksheet does not include four blank lines at the end, click once anywhere in the worksheet to select it, and use the* **DEL** *key once to delete it. Re-embed the correct range by following steps 20-23 in the previous activity (Activity 2.1).*

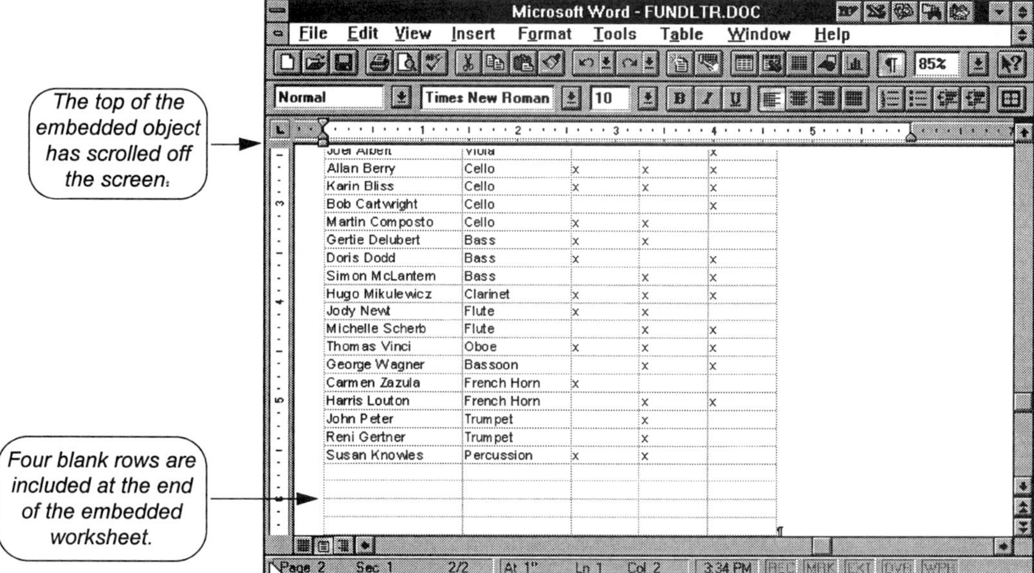

Figure 2 - 10 End of second embedded worksheet contains four blank lines

9. Click once on the embedded worksheet to select it.
10. Choose **EDIT/Spreadsheet (or Worksheet) Object, Open**.

Word will open Excel and place the embedded worksheet in a separate window titled ***Worksheet in FUNDLTR.DOC*** *(Figure 2 - 11). As the title bar indicates you are only editing* *the worksheet embedded in* ***fundltr.doc*** *not the original worksheet* ***expenses.xls****. You are now working totally in Excel but the changes you make will affect only the embedded worksheet. Notice that Excel has opened a copy of the entire* ***expenses.xls*** *worksheet. You have access to the entire worksheet (which you will use in calculations), but when you return to Word only the original range that you embedded will be visible.*

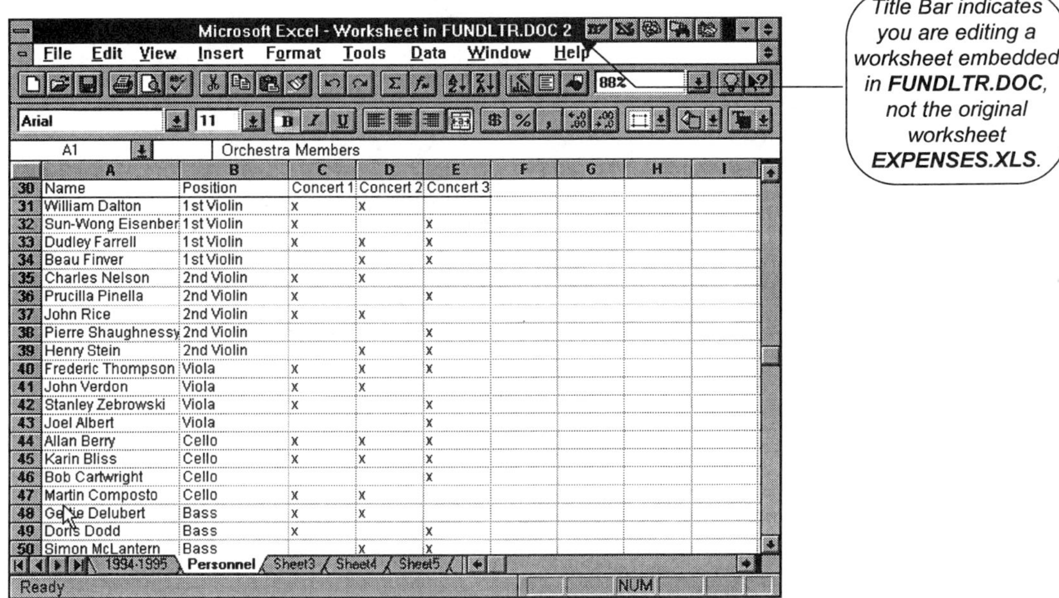

Figure 2 - 11 Embedded worksheet ready to be edited in separate *Excel* window

11. Maximize *Excel* and the worksheet window so that the worksheet is easier to edit.
12. Bold the column titles in row **30**.

    Now you are going to enter the formulas that will indicate the number of volunteer, paid, and total orchestra members and the percentage of the total that were volunteer.

13. Enter the following titles in the cells indicated:

    B61 **Total Volunteers**
    B62 **Total Paid**
    B63 **Total Orchestra**
    B64 **% Volunteers**

14. Since different people played in each of the concerts, to find the total volunteers for the first concert you must count the cells from **C31** to **C60** which contain an **X**. To do this:

    a. Select cell **C61**.

    b. Choose **INSERT/Function**.

    c. Choose **Statistical** from the **Function Category** list box.

    d. Scroll the **Function Name** list until you see both **COUNT** and **COUNTA. COUNT** only counts numbers. Since the cells you wish to count contain X's, you must use the **COUNTA** function (Figure 2 - 12).

    e. Click on **COUNTA** and then click on the **NEXT** button.

    The cursor will be in the ***Value1*** *box.*

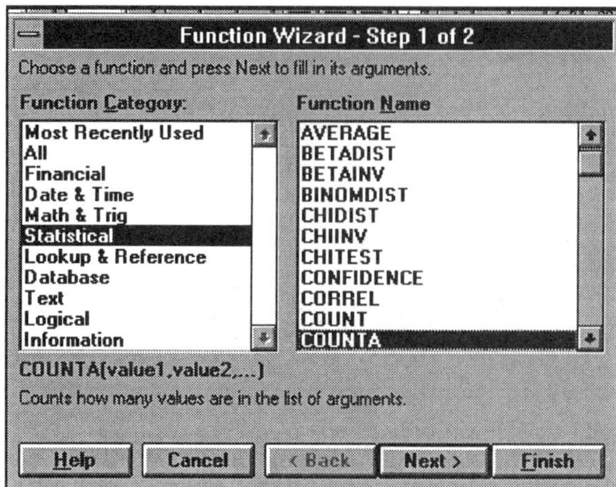

Figure 2 - 12 The Function Wizard dialog box with COUNTA selected

f. Select cells **C31:C60**.

HINT: *Move the* ***Function Wizard*** *box by dragging it by its title bar if necessary to see the cells you are selecting.*

The selected cells are surrounded by a moving border (Figure 2 - 13).

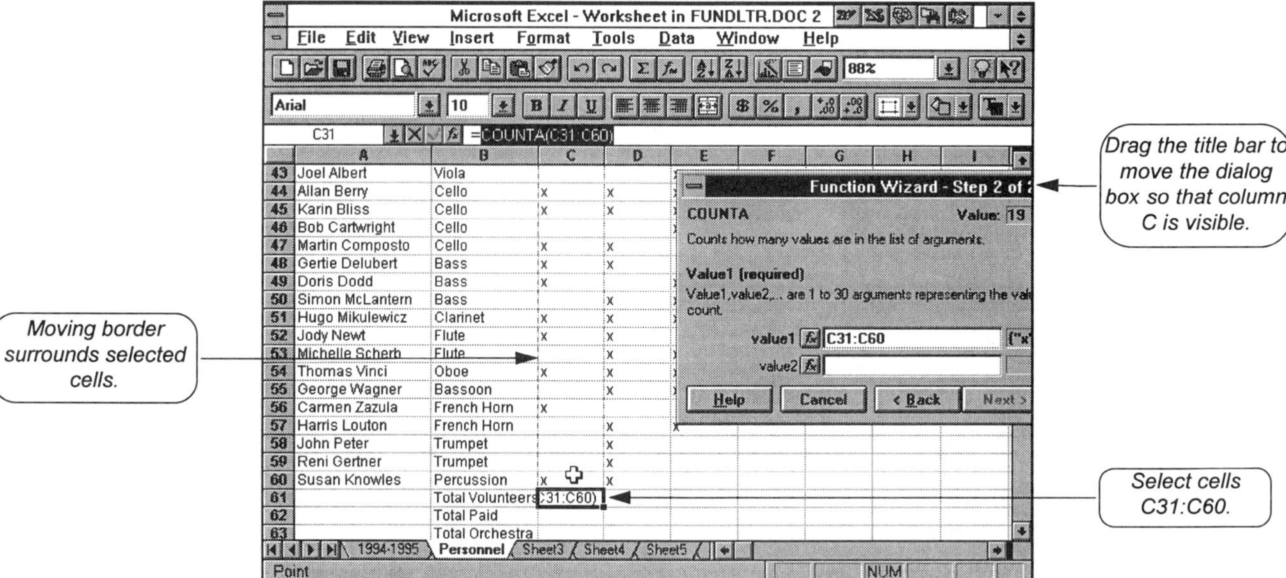

Figure 2 - 13 The completed Function Wizard dialog box

g. Click on **Finish** or press **ENTER**.

15. In cell **C62** use **COUNTA** to count the number of paid orchestra members (indicated by filled cells in the range **C9:C26**).
16. In cell **C63** enter a formula to sum the total number of volunteer and paid orchestra members.
17. In cell **C64** enter a formula to divide the total volunteers by the total orchestra.

When finished your worksheet should resemble Figure 2 - 14.

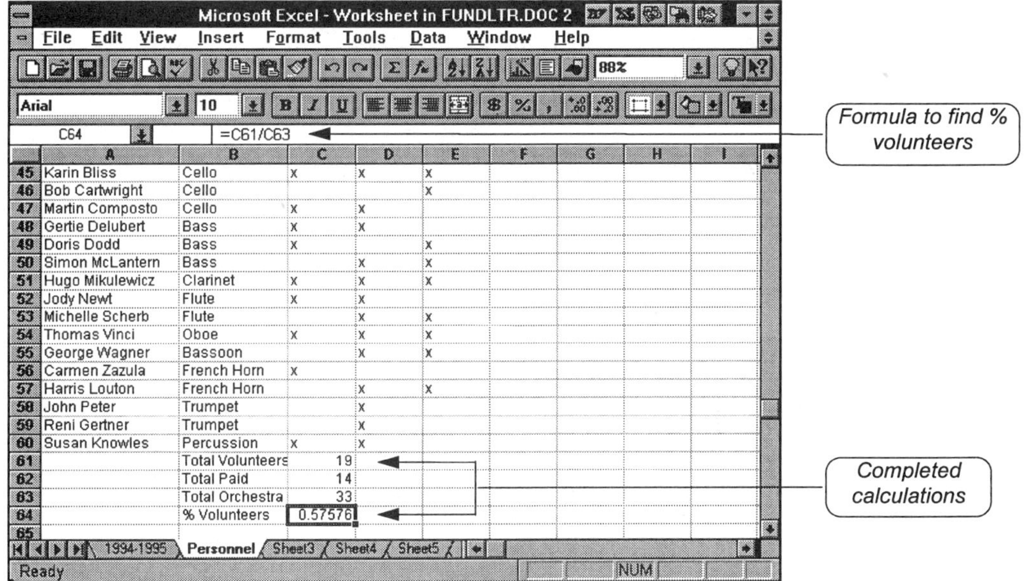

Figure 2 - 14 Worksheet with new calculations

18. Select cells **C61:C64** and copy the formulas to columns **D** and **E**.
19. Format the values in row **64** for **Percent** with no decimal places.

You've finished editing the worksheet. If your worksheet resembles Figure 2 - 15 you're ready to return to ***fundltr.doc****.*

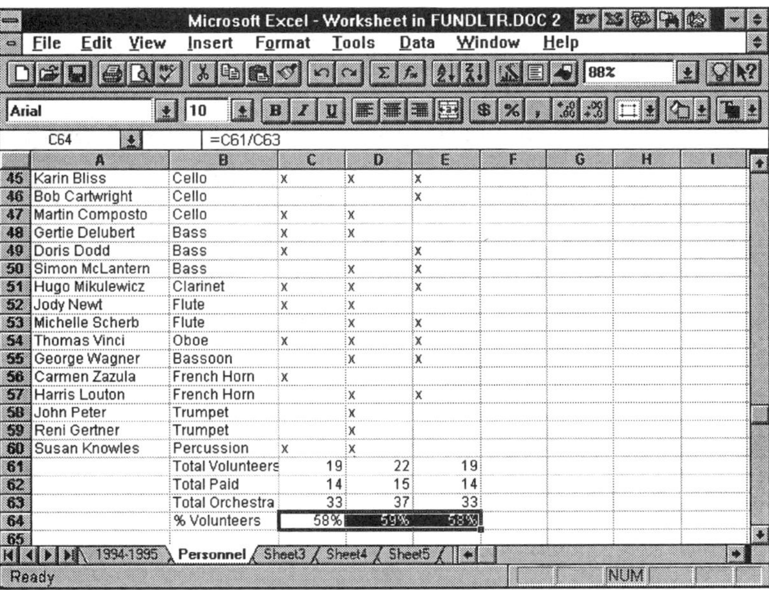

Figure 2 - 15 The edited worksheet

20. To update **fundltr.doc**, choose **FILE/Update**.
21. Choose **FILE/Exit** to close the worksheet and exit *Excel*.

NOTE: *Choosing* ***FILE/Close*** *will also return you to Word. We chose* ***FILE/Exit*** *to exit from Excel so that we would free some memory.*

22. Look at the end of the embedded worksheet to see that the new calculations have been included in the letter (Figure 2 - 16). Scroll to the beginning of page 2. The column headings, Name, Position, etc. should appear and should be bold.

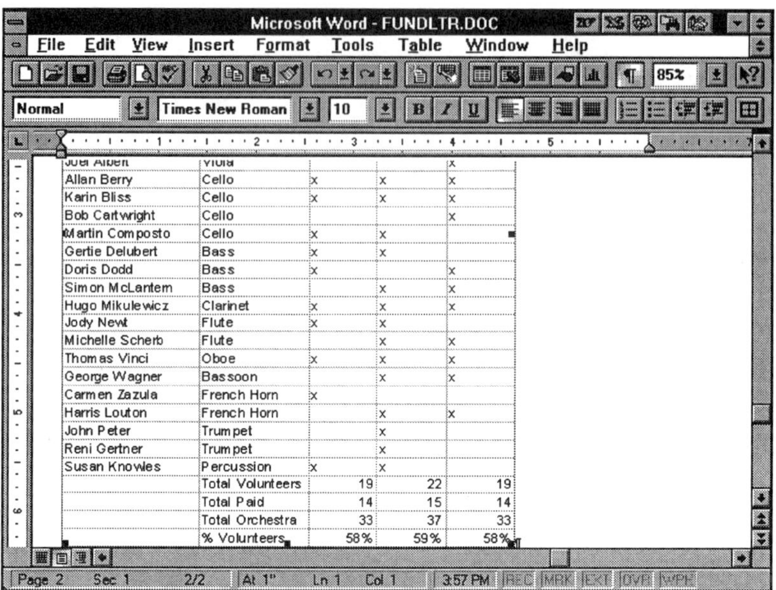

Figure 2 - 16 The editing changes appear in *Word*

23. Press **CTRL+END** to return to the end of the letter. If necessary use the scroll bar to scroll down the screen so that you can see the end of the document.

NOTE: ***CTRL+END*** *will not move you to the end of an embedded object unless there is a paragraph symbol or text following the embedded object.*

24. Press **ENTER** twice and type the final paragraphs and letter closing:

As you can see we have used a number of different volunteers and the orchestra for each concert has included more than 55% volunteer members.

We are very pleased with both the quality of our concerts and community involvement. Enclosed is our completed application for next year's funding. We hope that we can count on your continued support.

Sincerely,

(Your Name)

25. Spell check the letter.
26. Save the letter using the current name.
27. Print the letter.

HOW DID EDITING CHANGES AFFECT THE SOURCE DOCUMENT?

The answer to this question is the same as in Lesson 1 — editing the embedded object had *no* affect on the source document because the connection is between the embedded object and the source application, not the source document. That's why even when you edited the embedded worksheet in a full-size window within *Excel,* the title of the window was *Worksheet in*

FUNDLTR.DOC. If the editing procedure were going to change the original document, the title bar would have had the name of the original document, **expenses.xls**.

Activity 2.3: Seeing the Effect of Editing an Embedded Object on the Source Data and Vice Versa

As in Lesson 1, the main purpose of this activity is to let you prove to yourself that an embedded object and its source file have no connection — editing changes made to one do not affect the other.

1. Open *Excel* and **expenses.xls**.

   The column headings, Name, Position, etc., are not bold as they are in the embedded worksheets.

2. Scroll the worksheet so that rows **60** to **64** are visible.

   *Row **60** contains data on Susan Knowles. The other four rows are blank. None of the summary statistics that you added to the embedded worksheet were added to the original worksheet.*

3. Just to prove that changes to the source document don't affect the embedded document:

   a. Scroll to the beginning of the worksheet.

   b. Change **C8** to: **Fall Concert**

      Fall Concert is not fully visible. Don't worry, you'll change the alignment later.

   c. Change *Concert 2* to: **Winter Concert**

   d. Change *Concert 3* to: **Spring Concert**

   e. Select **C8:E8**.

   f. Choose **FORMAT/Cells,Alignment** and mark the **Wrap Text** check box. Choose **OK**.

      ***Expenses.xls** should now resemble Figure 2 - 17.*

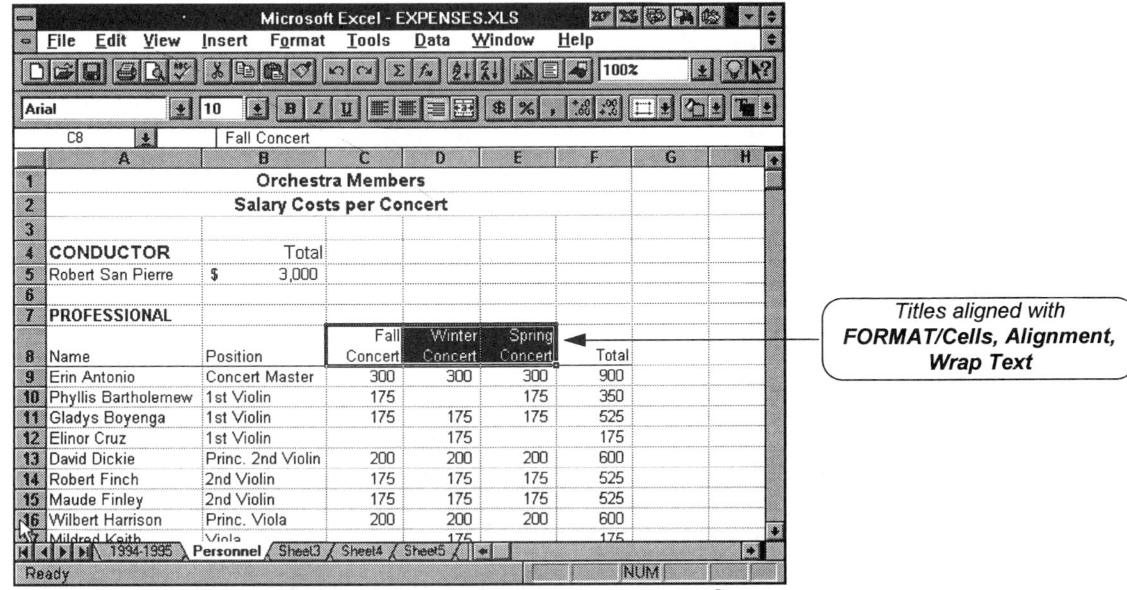

	A	B	C	D	E	F
1		Orchestra Members				
2		Salary Costs per Concert				
3						
4	CONDUCTOR	Total				
5	Robert San Pierre	$ 3,000				
6						
7	PROFESSIONAL					
8	Name	Position	Fall Concert	Winter Concert	Spring Concert	Total
9	Erin Antonio	Concert Master	300	300	300	900
10	Phyllis Bartholemew	1st Violin	175		175	350
11	Gladys Boyenga	1st Violin	175	175	175	525
12	Elinor Cruz	1st Violin		175		175
13	David Dickie	Princ. 2nd Violin	200	200	200	600
14	Robert Finch	2nd Violin	175	175	175	525
15	Maude Finley	2nd Violin	175	175	175	525
16	Wilbert Harrison	Princ. Viola	200	200	200	600
17	Mildred Keith	Viola		175		175

Figure 2 - 17 Editing changes in source document, expenses.xls.

4. Save **expenses.xls** using the existing name and exit from *Excel*.

5. Switch back to *Word* if it is not already on the screen.
6. Look at the embedded worksheet on page one of the letter. The changes to the concert names that you made in **expenses.xls** do not appear. If you wanted the changes to appear you would need to edit the embedded worksheet and repeat the steps that you just took to change the concert names. You could also delete the embedded worksheet, open *Excel* and **expenses.xls**, and recopy and re-embed **A8:E26**. However, if you did this, the changes that you made to the embedded worksheet in Activity 2.2 would be lost! In Lesson 3, you will learn to use linking to automatically update the destination document when the source is changed.
7. Close **fundltr.doc**.

EMBEDDING A NEW OBJECT

As we mentioned at the beginning of the lesson, it is also often useful to embed a new object. When you embed a new object you choose the application that would best handle the data and use the commands of that application to create the object. You'll see how helpful that can be in the next project in this lesson.

PROJECT 2 DESCRIPTION

In this project you, as chairperson of the Powell Community Orchestra board, are writing a memo to the rest of the board describing the terms of a proposed agreement to use the Woodlands Art Center Auditorium for next season's concerts. The beginning of the memo is included in **rent.doc**. At the point where you will continue the memo, you have decided to include a small calculation on how much additional subscription revenue the new concert site might bring to the orchestra. You guess that between 5% and 25% of the Woodlands Art Center members might buy orchestra subscriptions. You can use *Excel's* Fill Series feature to calculate the potential revenue generated by these extra subscriptions. You have not yet created a worksheet containing this information and you have no need to save the information as a stand-alone workbook. Therefore, you will insert a new *Microsoft Excel* worksheet object into your memo. When finished your memo will resemble Figure 2 - 18.

Memorandum

DATE: July 8, 1995

TO: Board of Trustees

FROM: Jessica Stand, Chairperson

RE: New auditorium for next season

Great news! The Woodlands Arts Center Board of Directors has agreed to let us use their new auditorium for next year's concerts. The fee will be $675 per concert which is $2,025 for our three subscription concerts. This is less than the $2,200 we are currently paying.

I also think that the advantages of this new arrangement will be far greater than the $175 savings in rent. The Woodlands Arts Center has a fine reputation for its dance productions and visual art exhibits. Association with the Arts Center will enhance our position in the community.

Our agreement might also increase our subscriptions. The Arts Center has agreed to let us mail to their 1,200 person membership list. I am estimating that between 5% and 25% of their members will subscribe to our concerts. You can see from the figures below how much this can add to our revenues!

% of Membership Subscribing:	5%	10%	15%	20%	25%
New Subscription Revenue:	$ 2,400	$ 4,800	$ 7,200	$ 9,600	$ 12,000

I hope that we can vote on the rental agreement at our next meeting.

Figure 2 - 18 The completed memo with new embedded worksheet object

STEPS IN EMBEDDING A NEW OBJECT

The **INSERT/Object** command is used to embed a new object.

To embed a new object:

- Position the insertion point at the location where you want to embed the object.
- Choose **INSERT/Object**.
- When the **Object** dialog box appears, choose the **Create New** tab if it is not already selected.

ALTERNATIVE METHOD: *The **Object** dialog box also contains a **Create from File** tab. As you might guess, this is another way of embedding an existing object. This differs from the way you used **Copy** and **Paste Special** in that the source application and file do not need to be open. However, the command attempts to display the entire object (or a part of the object that it determines, such as the sheet that was selected when you saved an Excel workbook). In Project 1 in this lesson if you had used **INSERT/Objects,Create from File** to embed **expenses.xls**, the entire worksheet would have been condensed and displayed in your memo in one place, whereas you wanted a part of the worksheet in one part of the letter and a second part later in the letter. You could have changed the display to get what you wanted, but the procedure you followed was easier.*

- Choose the type of object that you want to embed and click on **OK**.

  A window will open allowing you to use all the commands of the application selected to create the object. As when you edited an embedded object, either a small window will open within the application you are using and the menu bar, tool bars, etc. will change to that of the new application or a full-sized window separate from the destination application will appear.

- Create the embedded object.
- Use one of the methods you used after editing an embedded object to save your embedded object and return to the destination document:
  - Press **ESC** twice (in some situations, pressing once is enough) or click in the destination document window outside of the embedded object twice. These techniques work if the embedded object is in a small window within the destination document.
  - Or, if you are editing the embedded object in its own full-sized window, choose **FILE/Update** and then choose **FILE/Close** to close the document and return to the source application or **FILE/Exit** to close the application and return to the destination document. If the command **FILE/Exit and Return To (the destination application)** or **FILE/Close and Return to (the destination application)** appears on the **File** menu, use that command instead.

ALTERNATIVE METHOD: *The **INSERT MICROSOFT EXCEL WORKSHEET** button on the Standard toolbar can be used instead of **INSERT/Object** to insert a new Excel worksheet. After you click on the button, a grid appears. Drag across the grid to indicate the number of columns and rows that you wish to display in the worksheet.*

Activity 2.4: Embedding a New Worksheet in a Word Document

In this activity you will add to a memo to the Board of Trustees describing the conditions of the new lease. The file **rent.doc** stops at the point at which the chairperson of the Board of Trustees (you) wants to include a few calculations to show potential increased revenues that the new rental agreement might generate. To perform this calculation you will embed a new *Excel* worksheet.

1. Open *Word* if it is not running.
2. Open the file **rent.doc** which is on your data disk.
3. Read the document.
4. In the *FROM:* line of the memo replace *(your name)* with your name.
5. Move the insertion point to the end of the document.

   The cursor should be at the left margin on a blank line two lines below the last paragraph.
6. Type:

   Our agreement might also increase our subscriptions. The Arts Center has agreed to let us mail to their 1,200 person membership list. I am estimating that between 5% and 25% of their members will subscribe to our concerts. You can see from the figures below how much this can add to our revenues!
7. Press **ENTER** twice.

   Now you are ready to include a worksheet calculation to back up your last sentence!
8. Choose **INSERT/Object**.
9. The **Create New** tab should be selected. If it is not, click on it to select it (Figure 2 - 19).

   *The contents of the **Object Type** list on your computer might differ from Figure 2 - 19. During the installation of Office, it examines your hard drive and includes listings for the applications on your hard drive which can create objects which can be embedded in Word.*

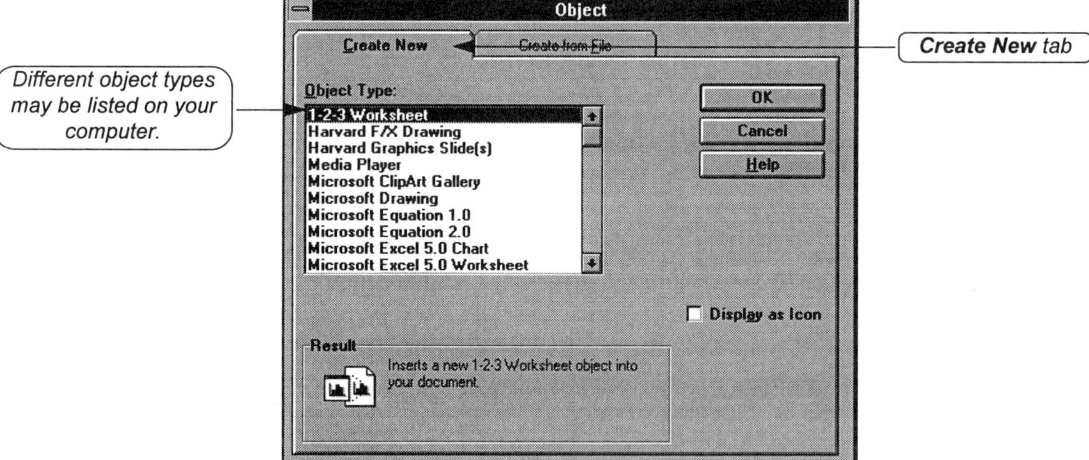

Figure 2 - 19 Object dialog box

10. Choose **Microsoft Excel 5.0 Worksheet** and click on **OK** or press **ENTER**.

    A small window of a worksheet should be displayed on your screen. The rest of the screen is the same as it was when you embedded a worksheet object in the last project — the title bar, one set of scroll bars and status bar belong to the Word document in which you are embedding the object. The menus, toolbars, second set of scroll bars, and Formula Bar belong to Excel (Figure 2 - 20).

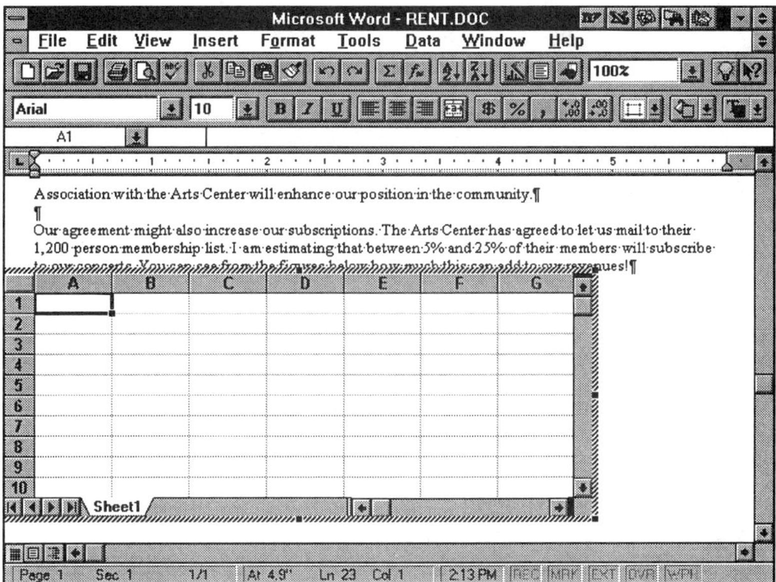

Figure 2 - 20 A new embedded worksheet object

11. In cell **A1** enter: **% of Membership Subscribing:**
12. In cell **A2** enter: **New Subscription Revenue:**
13. Increase the width of column **A** so that the two labels that you just typed fit.
14. In cell **B1** enter: **5%**
15. Select the range **B1:F1**.
16. Choose **EDIT/Fill, Series**.
17. The **Step Value** text box in the **Series** dialog box should be selected. Type: **5%** and press **ENTER** or click on **OK** (Figure 2 - 21).

    A series of percentages from 5% to 25% should be entered in cells ***B1:F1***.

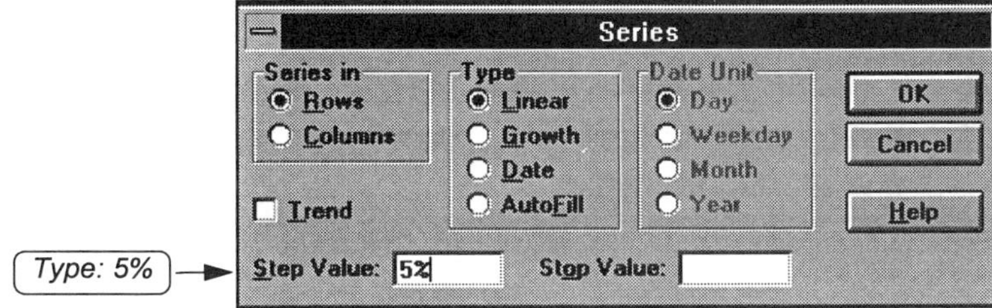

Figure 2 - 21 Series dialog box

18. In cell **B2** enter the formula to calculate the revenue from subscriptions if the percent of the membership in the row above subscribes. The formula should multiple **40** (the cost of a subscription) by **1200** (the number of adult members of the Arts Center) by the contents of cell **B1** (Figure 2 - 22).
19. Copy the formula in **B2** across row **2** through column **F.**

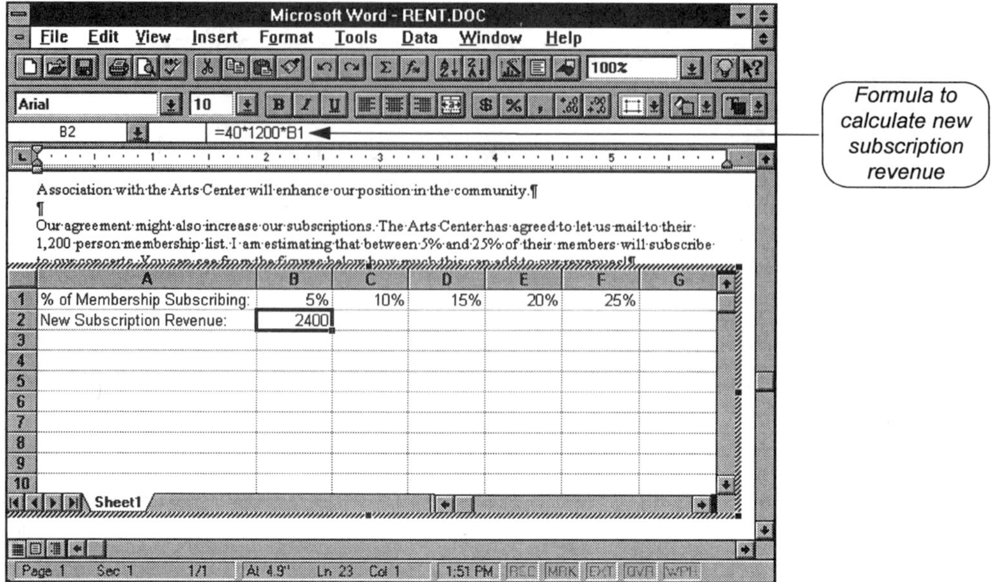

Figure 2 - 22 Adding a formula in B2

20. Format **B2:F2** for **Currency**, with zero decimal places.

    The worksheet Word embedded has many more rows than you need. Therefore, you need to decrease the size of the part of the embedded worksheet displayed.

21. Place the mouse pointer on the handle in the middle of the bottom frame of the worksheet (Figure 2 - 23). When the pointer changes to a ↕ , drag the border up so that the two completed rows of the worksheet will be displayed. (You may need to repeat this a few times until the correct part of the worksheet is displayed.)

PROBLEM SOLVER: *If you accidentally click outside of the Excel window, you will end editing. Double-click anywhere in the worksheet to return to the Excel window.*

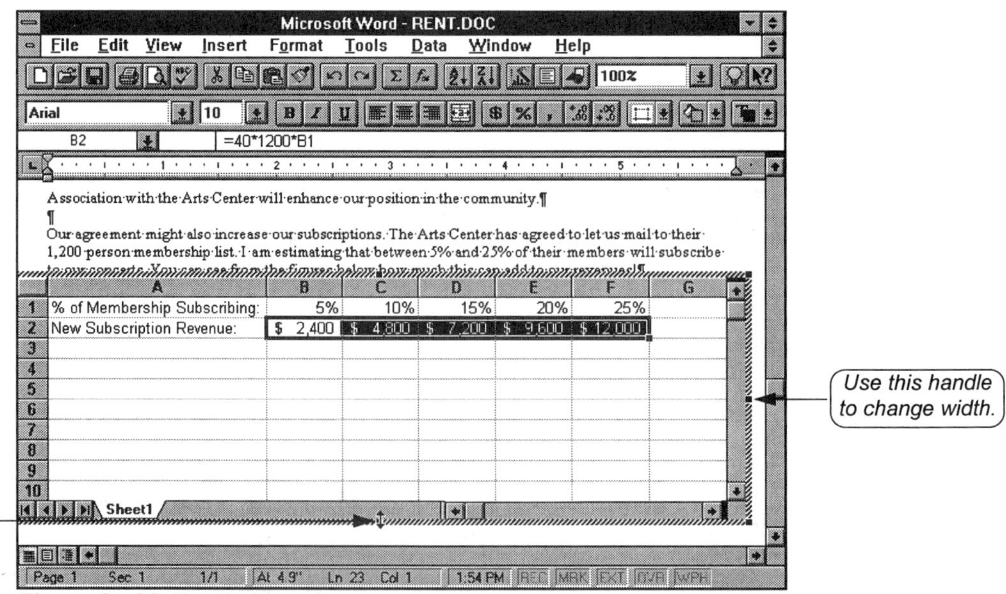

Figure 2 - 23 Ready to resize

22. Decrease the width of the worksheet so that column **G** is not displayed (if it is currently displayed on your screen).

    The screen should resemble Figure 2 - 24.

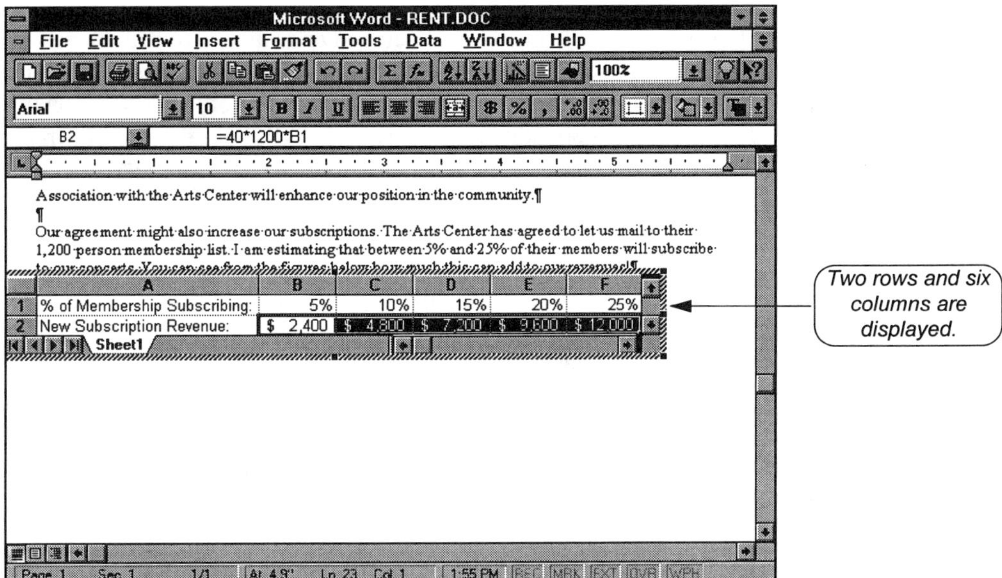

Figure 2 - 24 Resized embedded worksheet window

ALTERNATIVE METHOD: *This same procedure can be used to increase or decrease the amount of an embedded object from an existing file which is displayed. For example in Project 1 you could have just copied and embedded the worksheet rows that contained data and then used this procedure to expand the worksheet area to include space for the new calculations.*

23. Press **ESC** once and click once outside of the worksheet, or click twice on the *Word* screen outside of the embedded worksheet.
24. Press **ENTER** twice.
25. Type: **I hope that we can vote on the rental agreement at our next meeting.**
26. Spell check the letter.
27. Save the file using the name: **rentfin.doc**
28. You are about to print the letter when you decide that the row labels in column **A** would be clearer if they were bold. To change the format you edit the embedded worksheet just as you did an existing worksheet object. In this example, the worksheet is small so you can double-click on it to edit. However, the **EDIT/Spreadsheet (Worksheet) Object,Open** editing option can also be used.
    a. Double-click anywhere on the embedded worksheet object.
    b. Select cells **A1:A2**.
    c. Click on the **BOLD** button on the Formatting toolbar.
    d. Increase the width of column **A** so that the entire row titles fit in the column.
29. Click twice in *Word* outside of the worksheet window.
30. Save the file using the current name.

31. Print the letter.
32. Close the file. Go on to Independent Activity 2.1 or exit from *Word*.

SUMMARY

In this lesson you have learned how to embed and edit existing and new worksheet objects in *Word* documents. In the process you have seen the most important difference between pasting and embedding — pasted objects are edited using the tools of the destination application while embedded documents are edited using the tools of the application that created the object (the source application). These similarities and differences are summarized below.

Similarities between pasting and embedding objects:

- The object is part of the destination document and is saved with that document.
- The object does not change when the source data is edited and the source data does not change when the pasted or embedded object is changed.
- The file containing the pasted or embedded object is easy to transport from computer to computer because the pasted or embedded object is actually part of the file.

Differences between pasting and embedding objects:

Pasted Object	Embedded Object
• Only the text and formatting are copied to the destination document (i.e., a pasted worksheet contains numbers in place of any formulas that were contained in the original). Formatting may be modified to conform with formatting options of the destination application.	• All aspects of the original object are present in the destination document (i.e., an embedded worksheet contains all of the formulas in the original).
• Increase in file size is approximately equal to increase that would be caused by entering the formatted text directly into the document.	• Increase is file size is much larger than that accounted for by the formatted text; the entire source file and all of the information needed to edit the object in the source application are stored in the destination file.
• The pasted data is edited using the commands of the destination application.	• The object is edited using the commands of the source application.
• The source application does *not* need to be present in order to edit the pasted data.	• The source application must be on the computer in order to edit the object.
• The destination file contains only the part of the source file copied and pasted into it.	• The destination file contains the entire source file although only the part you copied and embedded will appear.

In the independent activities you will practice embedding *Excel* worksheet objects into *Word* and extend these skills to embedding different objects (charts, *Word* tables) into a different application (*PowerPoint)*.

KEY TERMS

Bitmap	New Object	Unformatted Text
Existing Object	Picture	
Formatted Text (RTF)	Spreadsheet Object	

INDEPENDENT PROJECTS

Independent Project 2.1: Embedding an Existing Excel Worksheet Range and an Excel Chart into a Word Document

In this project you will return to Dan's Sport Shop and see why you might have wanted to embed the data from **regsales.xls** into **danmemo.xls** rather than paste it. In Independent Project 1.1, after you pasted the worksheet data, the only changes that you made to it involved formatting and making a minor change to some of the text. On rethinking the memo, however, you decide that since the memo is focusing on the Northern region vs. the other regions, you want to include some additional calculations which compare sales in this region to sales in the other regions. In order to do these calculations you need to use *Excel*'s commands so you will embed rather than paste the worksheet data into the memo. As you will see in the next lesson, linking the data would also give you access to *Excel,* but any changes made to the data would also change the source document. The extra calculations do not belong in the original worksheet so linking would not be a good option in this activity. When completed, your memo should resemble Figure 2 - 25.

1. Start Microsoft Office, if necessary. Open *Word.*
2. Open **danmemo.doc**.

   This is the same memo you used in Independent Project 1.1. It should only include the memo heading and the first paragraph of the memo.

   PROBLEM SOLVER: *If you accidentally saved your completed project as* ***danmemo.doc*** *instead of* ***2ndqdan.doc****, delete all of the tables and text after the first paragraph.*

3. Move the insertion point to the end of the memo.
4. Open *Excel* and **regsales.xls**.
5. If the **2nd Quarter** sheet is not active, click on the **2nd Quarter** tab on the horizontal scroll bar.
6. Select the range **A8:F15**.
7. Copy the selected range.
8. Switch to **danmemo.doc**.
9. Use **EDIT/Paste Special** to embed the **Microsoft Excel 5.0 Worksheet Object**.
10. **Save** the file **as: northern.doc**

Before finishing the memo you decide that you want to perform some more calculations to see the relationship between sales in the Northern region and average sales of the same products.

11. The embedded worksheet should be approximately centered on the screen. If it is not scroll the document so that the embedded worksheet is approximately centered between the top and bottom of the document window. This will make it easier to edit.
12. Double-click on the worksheet so that you can begin editing it using *Excel.*

   CAUTION: *Remember, once the Excel window appears, be careful NOT to scroll the worksheet within the Excel window, as whatever is visible in the Excel window when you are finished editing the worksheet will be displayed in the memo.*

MEMORANDUM

TO: DAN WHITE
Manager, Dan's Sport Shop, Inc.

FROM: LAURA MICHAELS
Financial Advisor

RE: Preliminary Second Quarter Regional Sales Figures

I've just finished my preliminary look at the second quarter regional sales figures and thought you would want to see them right away. I focused on the Northern region as you requested. The table below includes the sales figures summarized by product and region.

PRODUCT	EASTERN	WESTERN	NORTHERN	SOUTHERN	AVERAGE	NORTH DIFF.
Baseball Bats	$10,500	$5,467	$7,000	$6,000	$7,242	($242)
Golf Club Sets	9,975	7,555	7,000	9,887	$8,604	($1,604)
Kayaks	3,500	9,999	7,221	9,600	$7,580	($359)
Tennis Racquets	6,522	6,700	17,000	7,700	$9,481	$7,520
Boxing Gloves	8,800	1,234	3,300	6,600	$4,984	($1,684)
Scuba Gear	8,330	5,200	7,300	9,900	$7,683	($383)
Totals	$47,627	$36,155	$48,821	$49,687	$45,573	$3,249

The chart of the sales data which follows highlights some of the sales differences.

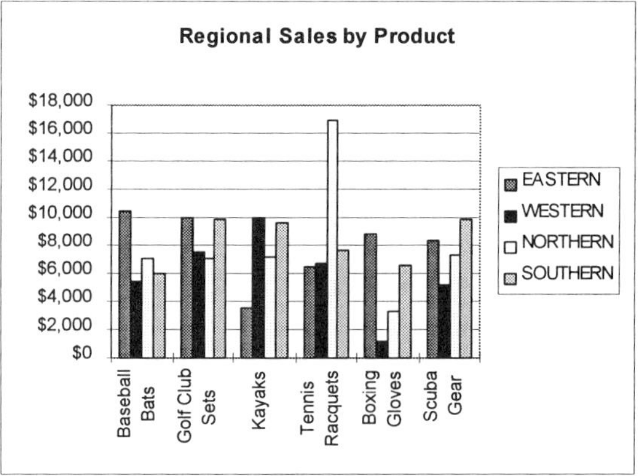

Sales for tennis racquets in the Northern region were higher than for any other product in any region. In fact these sales were so high that total sales for the Northern region were $3,249 over the average regional sales. However, sales for all other products in the Northern region were less than the average sales for that product. I propose that we conduct a small market research study to see if we can isolate reasons for the unexpectedly high sales of tennis racquets, and determine which of the other products should be doing better than they are in this region.

Figure 2 - 25 Completed project

13. Select **F8:F15** and press the **DEL** key to clear the contents from the range without removing the formatting.
14. Click in **F8** and enter the new column heading: **AVERAGE**
15. In **F9** enter the function for calculating the average sales of baseball bats in the four regions: **=average(B9:E9)**
16. Copy the formula down through row **15**.

You want to add a column comparing sales in the Northern region with the average sales for each product and the total. To do this you must first expand the size of the Excel worksheet that is visible.

17. Point the handle in the middle of the right side of the *Excel* window frame. When the pointer changes to a ↔ drag it approximately one column width to the right (Figure 2 - 26).

    Column G should now be visible in the worksheet.

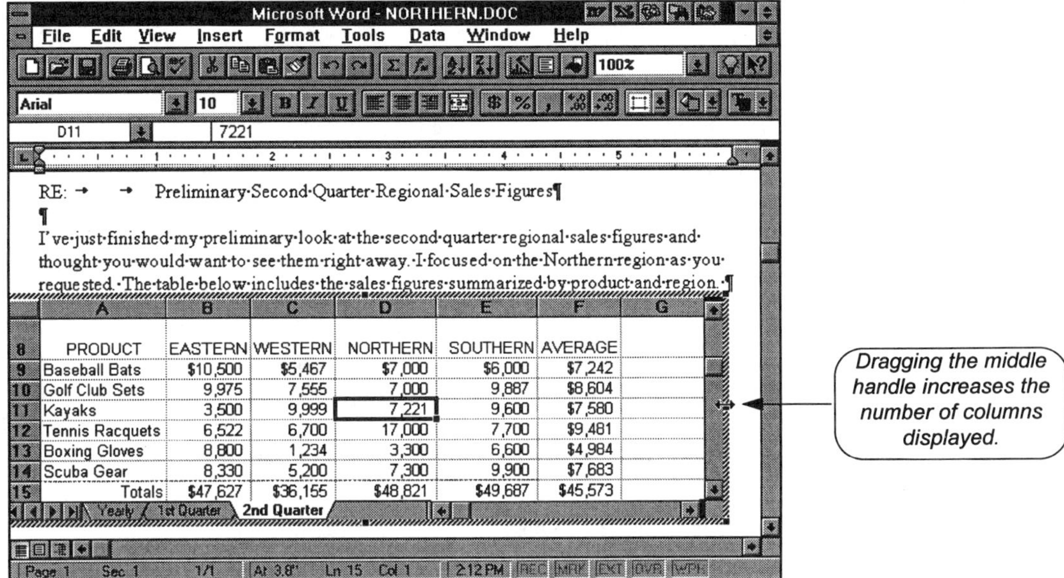

Figure 2 - 26 Adding a column to the embedded worksheet

18. In cell **G8** enter: **NORTH DIFF.**
19. Select **G8** if it is not still selected and choose **FORMAT/Cells,Alignment**. Change the horizontal alignment to **Right** and mark the **Wrap Text** check box to display the title right-justified on two lines. Choose **OK**.
20. In **G9** enter a formula to subtract the average sales for baseball bats from the Northern sales for baseball bats. (**HINT:** Your answer should be negative since the average sales for baseball bats was greater than the sales in the Northern region.)
21. Copy the formula down column **G** through row **15**.
22. Select **F14:G14**.
23. Choose **FORMAT/Cells,Border**. Click on the dashed line **Style** (second from top on right-side of **Style** box) and click on the **Bottom** border (Figure 2 - 27). Click on **OK**. The border of the two new cells now matches the original border.

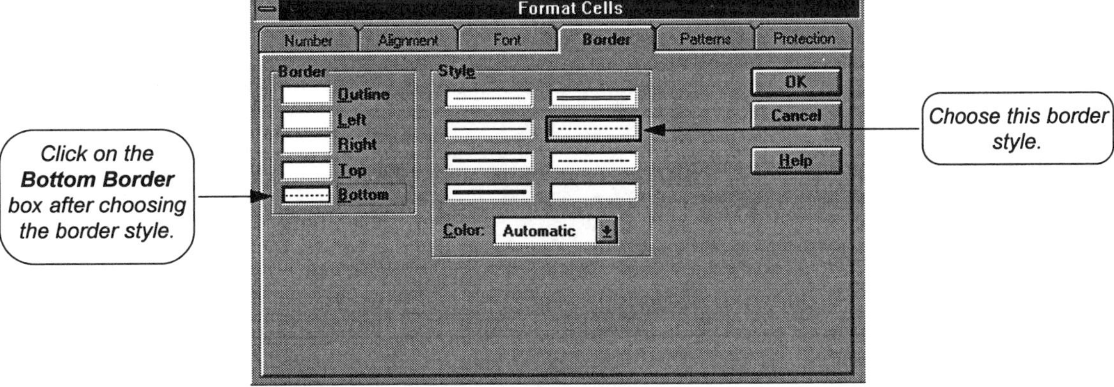

Figure 2 - 27 Completed border dialog box

24. Be sure that row **8** is the first row visible in the *Excel* window. If it is not, scroll the worksheet until it is.
25. Press **ESC** and click once outside of the worksheet, or click twice outside of the worksheet.
26. If the embedded worksheet extends into the margin, click on it once so that it is surrounded by handles. (Do NOT double-click. You must be in *Word* not in the *Excel* editing window.) Click on the middle handle on the right side of the embedded worksheet and drag it until the right side of the embedded worksheet approximately lines up with the memo text.
27. Save the memo again using the current name.
28. Move the insertion point to the end of the document and press **ENTER**.
29. Type:

    Sales for tennis racquets in the Northern region were higher than for any other product in any region. In fact these sales were so high that total sales for the Northern region were $3,249 over the average regional sales. However, sales for all other products in the Northern region were less than the average sales for that product. I propose that we conduct a small market research study to see if we can isolate reasons for the unexpectedly high sales of tennis racquets, and determine which of the other products should be doing better than they are in this region.

30. Spell check the document.
31. Save the document again using the current name.
32. Print the document.

    After reading the memo you decide that the sales results would be even clearer if you include a chart of the sales. You will see that *Word* makes you embed rather than paste the chart in the *Word* document because charts cannot be edited using *Word* commands.

33. Move the insertion point to the blank line between the embedded *Excel* worksheet and the paragraph which follows it.
34. Press **ENTER**.
35. Type:

    The chart of the sales data which follows highlights some of the sales differences.

36. Press **ENTER** three times.
37. Move the insertion point to the middle blank line so that the chart will be inserted with blank lines on top and bottom of it.
38. Switch back to **regsales.xls**.
39. Scroll the horizontal scroll bar until the chart in columns **H:N** is visible (Figure 2 - 28).
40. Click once anywhere in the chart to select it.

    Handles will appear at the corners and middle of the sides of the chart when it is selected.

41. Copy the chart.
42. Switch to *Word*. Make sure the insertion point is on a blank line after the sentence describing the chart.
43. Choose **EDIT/Paste Special**.

    *Notice that the **As:** box indicates that the chart would be pasted as a **Microsoft Excel 5.0 Chart Object** (Figure 2 - 29). The **Result** box confirms that this is a document which can be edited in Microsoft Excel. Since the chart format is not native to Word, Office automatically embeds a chart even if you choose **EDIT/Paste.***

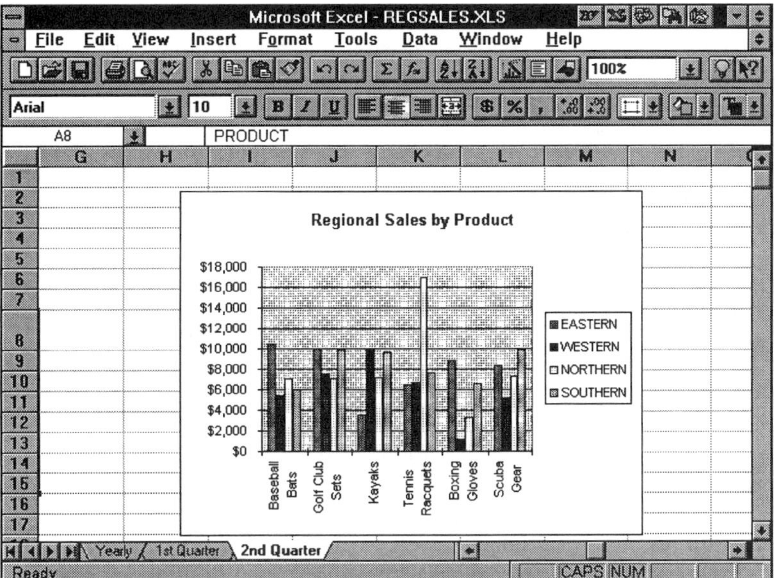

Figure 2 - 28 Chart on 2nd Quarter Sheet

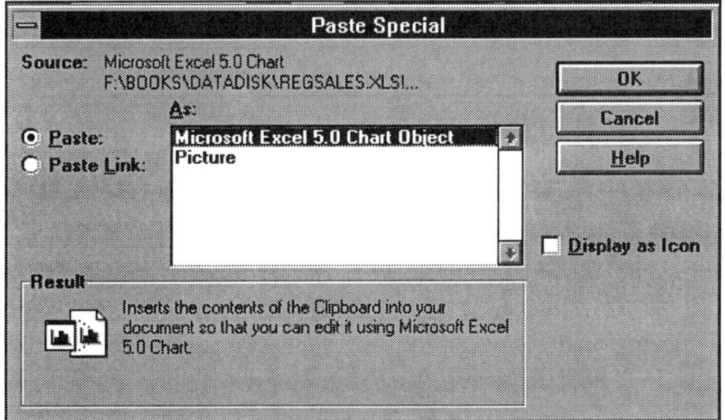

Figure 2 - 29 The *Word* Paste Special dialog box for a copied *Excel* chart

44. Choose **OK** to embed the object as a **Microsoft Excel 5.0 Chart Object**.
45. Click once on the chart to select it.
46. Click on the **CENTER** button on the toolbar to center the chart.
47. Scroll through the memo and make sure there is one blank line between paragraphs or paragraphs and objects. Add or delete blank lines as necessary.
48. Save the file again using the current name.
49. Print the memo.
50. Exit from *Word* and *Excel* without saving the *Excel* file.

Independent Project 2.2: Embedding a Word Table in a PowerPoint Presentation

As treasurer of the Powell Community Orchestra, you want to prepare a presentation on fiscal activities for the Annual Meeting. You have already written a memo to the Board of Trustees regarding fundraising activities, and you would like to include a table from this memo in the presentation. Since tables cannot be edited using *PowerPoint* commands, you must embed rather than paste the *Word* table. Because font sizes used in presentations are typically larger than those used in memos, you will need to increase the font size of the embedded table. This change should only affect the *PowerPoint* slide (not the original *Word* document) so the table must be embedded rather than linked. As you will learn in the next lesson, if you linked the *Word* table, the only way to change the font size in *PowerPoint* would be to also change it in *Word.* Figure 2 - 30 shows the *PowerPoint* slide with the edited, embedded *Word* table.

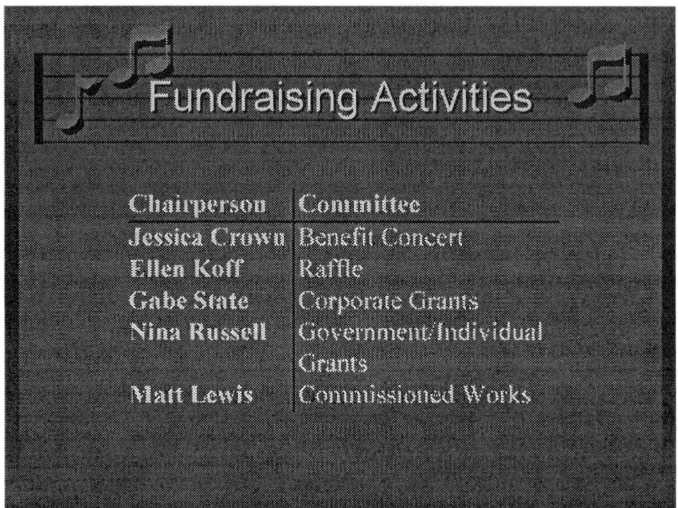

Figure 2 - 30 Completed *PowerPoint* slide

1. Start *Microsoft Office*, if necessary. Use the *Microsoft Office* toolbar to open *Word.*
2. Open the **fundrais.doc** file.
3. Select the first two columns of the table. (**HINT:** Place the mouse pointer slightly above the first column. When it turns into a thick down arrow, click and drag it to select the first and second columns.)
4. Choose **EDIT/Copy**.
5. Use the Microsoft Office toolbar to open *PowerPoint.*
6. Open the **fundrais.ppt** presentation from your data disk.
7. Move to Slide 3 (the last slide in the presentation).
8. Choose **EDIT/Paste Special**.
9. **Paste** and **Microsoft Word 6.0 Document Object** should be selected. If they are not, choose them and click on **OK**.

   Microsoft Word 6.0 Document Object *is selected instead of* ***Formatted Text (RFT)****. Because PowerPoint cannot edit tables, any Word table will automatically be embedded into PowerPoint rather than simply pasted.*

   The text is too small to read so you will increase the size of the text. You will also edit the format of the table and the color of the text.

10. Double-click on the *Word* table.

    You remain in PowerPoint. However, the menu bar and toolbars have changed to those in Word. You will edit the Word table using the commands of the source application while still remaining in PowerPoint, the destination application.

11. Click on the middle handle on the right-side of the *Word* window and drag it out until the ruler extends approximately to 6.5 inches.
12. Choose **TABLE/Select Table.**
13. Use the ruler at the top of the table to make the following formatting changes:
    - Drag the column marker at the right of Column 2 to increase the right margin of the table to **6.5** or to the object border.
    - Drag the column marker at the right of Column 1 to move the right margin of Column 1 to **2.5**.
14. Increase the size of the text to **28 pt**.
15. Increase the size of the object by dragging the middle handle of the bottom border down until all 6 rows of the table are visible.
16. While the table is still selected, choose **TABLE/Table AutoFormat**.
17. Choose the **Simple2** format and choose **OK**.
18. Return to the *PowerPoint* presentation by clicking once outside the *Word* table.

    Unlike when you copied and pasted text from Word to Excel, the color of the text remains black rather than changing to the default color of the presentation template. Therefore, you must change the color of the text.
19. Double-click on the *Word* table to edit it in *Word.*
20. Choose **TABLE/Select Table.**
21. Choose **FORMAT/Font.** Open the **Color** drop-down list box and choose **yellow**. Click on **OK**. The text will not appear yellow while the text is still selected.
22. Return to the *PowerPoint* presentation.
23. Click on the table once and drag it up so that it is centered on the slide.
24. Use the Microsoft Office toolbar to switch to *Word.*

    You return to the source document. Notice that the two original columns are still selected and none of the changes you just made have been applied to the source document.
25. Close *Word* without saving **fundrais.doc**.

    You will return to the PowerPoint presentation.
26. Save the presentation as **funrais2.ppt**.
27. Print Slide 3 using the **Black & White** option.
28. Close the presentation and exit *PowerPoint.*

Independent Project 2.3: Embedding a New Word 6.0 Object in an Excel Worksheet

There are several ways to include blocks of text in *Excel* worksheets. You can create a text box or add a note to a cell. However, the text entry capabilities of *Excel* are limited. If for example, you wanted to include information in a bulleted or numbered list, it would be far easier to embed a *Word* object and use the **NUMBERING** or **BULLETS** buttons to let you automatically create indented, well-formatted bulleted or numbered lists.

In this project you will once again use **expenses.xls**. This time you will look at the **1994-1995** sheet instead of the **Personnel** sheet that you have used before. The **1994-1995** sheet contains a very simple accounting of the Powell Community Orchestra's expenses for the 1994-1995 season.

You want to include a bulleted list directly on the worksheet to explain some of the expenses listed. To do this you will embed a *Word 6.0 object* so that you can use all of *Word*'s editing and formatting commands to create your bulleted list.

When completed the worksheet will resemble Figure 2 - 31.

Powell Community Orchestra	
1994-1995 Expenses	
Category	**Amount**
Conductor	3,000
Soloists	3,900
Personnel	8,350
Hall	2,200
Lighting	765
Hospitality	1,000
Insurance	350
Printing	2,000
Publicity	500
Postage	900
Fees	700
Music	850
Other	650
Total	$ 25,165

Explanation of expenses:

- Conductor and personnel expenses are for the three subscription concerts only.
- Soloists were used in the three subscription concerts plus the benefit.
- Hospitality expenses are low because Gourmet Food, Inc. donated the food for two concerts.
- Fees include membership in ASCAP, BMI and American Symphony Orchestra League.

Figure 2 - 31 Completed worksheet with embedded *Word* document

1. Start Microsoft Office, if necessary. Open *Excel.*
2. Open **expenses.xls**.
3. If the **1994-1995** sheet is not active click on the **1994-1995** sheet tab.
4. Click in cell **D5**.
5. Use **INSERT/Object** to insert a **Microsoft Word 6.0 document.**

   A small Word window will open within Excel. Notice that the title bar indicates you are working with a document in ***expenses.xls****. The menus and toolbars have changed to Word's (Figure 2 - 32). Unfortunately the Word window extends beyond the visible part of the Excel worksheet, so before you enter text you will decrease its size. You also need to make the Word window longer so that you can include more than one line of text.*

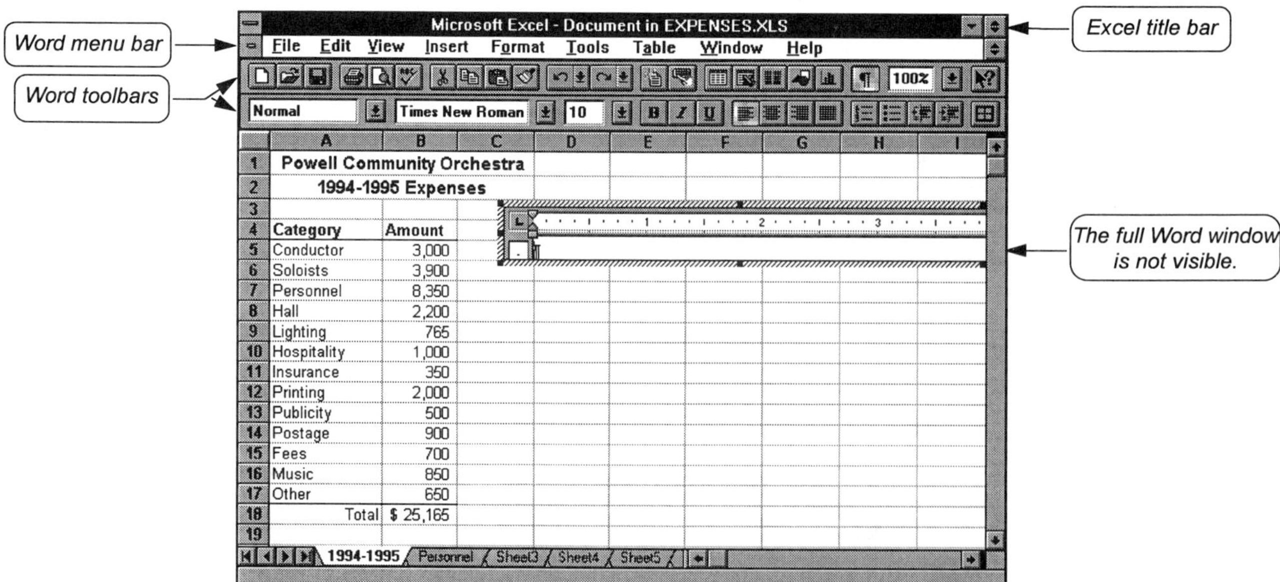

Figure 2 - 32 Inserting a new Word 6.0 object into an Excel worksheet

6. Scroll the screen so that you can see the right side on the *Word* window.
7. Click on the handle in the middle of the right side of the frame and drag it until the frame ends on the line between columns **G** and **H**.
8. Use the middle handle on the bottom frame to extend the bottom border down to the line between rows **18** and **19**.
9. Press the **SPACE BAR** once and then type:

   Explanation of expenses:

10. Press **ENTER** once.

11. Click on the **BULLETS** button on the *Word* Formatting toolbar.

12. Click on the **INCREASE INDENT** button on the *Word* Formatting toolbar to indent the bullet one-half inch.
13. Type the following items pressing **ENTER** after each bulleted item:
    - **Conductor and personnel expenses are for the three subscription concerts only.**
    - **Soloists were used in the three subscription concerts plus the benefit.**
    - **Hospitality expenses are low because Gourmet Foods, Inc. donated food for two concerts.**
    - **Fees include membership in ASCAP, BMI and American Symphony Orchestra League.**
14. Spell check the document.
15. Click on the worksheet outside of the *Word* window once.
16. Select cells **A1:G2**. Click on the **ALIGN LEFT** button and then the **CENTER ACROSS COLUMNS** button on the *Excel* toolbar.

    *The two-line worksheet title should be centered across columns **A:G**.*

17. **Save** the file **as**: **expense2.xls**
18. Print the sheet.
19. Close the file and exit from *Excel*.

Lesson 3

Linking Objects

Objectives

In this chapter you will learn how to:

- Define object linking
- Understand the advantages and disadvantages of using linked files
- Link an *Excel* worksheet range with a *Word* document
- Link an *Excel* chart with a *Word* document
- Edit linked files
- Update linked files
- Modify or repair links
- Link an *Excel* worksheet with a *PowerPoint* presentation
- Link an *Excel* chart with a *PowerPoint* presentation

PROJECT DESCRIPTION

In Lesson 3, you will explore the methods and consequences of *linking* data. In this project you, as the treasurer of the Powell Community Orchestra, will draft a memo in *Word for Windows*, reporting to the members of the Finance Committee on sources of income for the orchestra for the years 1991-1994. The data will come from an *Excel* worksheet.

Unfortunately, the worksheet data is incomplete, and in some cases wrong. You want to continue to correct the worksheet as more data becomes available, and you do not want to have to make the same corrections to the *Word* file. Thanks to *object linking*, the *Word* memo can be automatically updated as the *Excel* worksheet changes. Only when the worksheet data is finalized will you print and distribute the *Word* memo.

You will be *linking* the worksheet range and chart with the *Word* memo. Each time you edit the *Excel* source document, you will see how the links update. Then you will *rename* the source document and see how renaming affects the links that have been established. Finally, you will examine links that have been broken to see how they may be repaired. Figure 3 - 1 is a picture of the completed memo.

WHAT DOES OBJECT LINKING MEAN?

Instead of sharing data through *copying and pasting* or *embedding*, you may choose to *link* your data to another document. In the process called *object linking,* the link is a connection between two files, the source and the destination. The link itself is a code that is placed in the destination file, telling that file exactly what data to display, and in what format the data is to appear. Instructions for updating the link are also included. The linked data never becomes a part of the destination file as it does when the data is embedded — it remains in the source. Thus, the destination file is never enlarged by the addition of new data and commands for editing it. If you are working with a document that contains a great number of pictures, the file quickly becomes enormous if the pictures are embedded. Linking the pictures keeps the destination file size smaller

Powell Community Orchestra
Memorandum

DATE: January 16, 1995

TO: Finance Committee Members

FROM: Nancy Logan, Treasurer

RE: Analysis of Sources of Income

At our last meeting, Marge asked if we were seeing any trends in the sources of our income. I have put together the following data to help us analyze that question. Please examine this spreadsheet and chart before our meeting next week (January 21) so we can discuss this together. Thanks.

Powell Community Orchestra				
Sources of Income: 1991 - 1994				
	1991	1992	1993	1994
Contributed Income	$ 7,500	$ 8,575	$ 6,700	$ 7,600
Grant Income	$ 3,000	$ 3,500	$ 2,500	$ 2,000
Subscription Income	$ 9,000	$ 9,300	$ 9,700	$ 9,900
Earned Income	$ 1,650	$ 2,400	$ 3,400	$ 3,750
Total	$ 21,150	$ 23,775	$ 22,300	$ 23,250

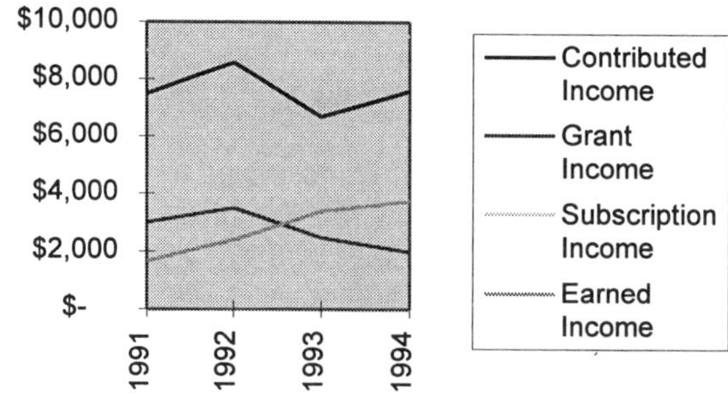

Please note that this data has been compiled by *calendar year*, not by season. It will not match your 1993-94 budget report

Figure 3 - 1 Completed version of the document

and makes the file less cumbersome. This book, *Getting Started with Microsoft Office*, was written in *Word 6.0 for Windows*. The text and pictures for each lesson were saved on a network, in different files and directories, and were connected by object linking.

You will see the advantage of linking over embedding whenever you want the source and destination files to remain identical. As you saw in Lesson 2, when data is embedded, the source and destination files are no longer connected, and must be edited separately, involving much time and effort as well as increased likelihood of errors and inconsistencies. When files are linked, you edit the source *only*. The links will be updated automatically or at your command, depending on the option you have chosen. Thus, with a minimum of labor you can ensure that your information is up-to-date and consistent.

However linking does have disadvantages. Never lose sight of the fact that a link is an ongoing connection between two documents. It is easy for links to become damaged or broken without the user becoming aware of it. The link specifies the identity and location of the linked data; if that information changes in any way, the link will not function properly. In addition, the user must have continual access to both the source and the linked documents and their applications for the link to work. In contrast, once you have embedded data, the source file is no longer connected to the destination document in any way.

When a file contains links, you will notice that it takes more time to open, save, and close it. This is particularly noticeable if the file has been saved to a floppy disk.

Paste Linking between *Excel* and *Word*

As we begin our project, let's return to the questions we have been asking in each lesson:

- Do I expect the source data to change? If it changes, do I want the data in the destination document to automatically change also?

  Yes, you do expect the source data to change. Remember that the 1994 data is incomplete and in some cases wrong. You will correct the data as better information becomes available.

- Will I need to edit the data once it is in the destination document? If so, do I want to use the source application or the destination application to do the editing? If I want to use the source application for the editing, is it available on the computer that will be used to edit the destination document?

  You want the data in the destination document to be identical to the original data. Therefore, you want to edit only once — in the source document. Then, you want the editing changes to be automatically updated in the destination document. The memo will not be distributed to the Finance Committee until all the editing changes have been made. The source application and document will both be available to you.

Use object linking if:

- Both the source and destination documents will need to change if the source data changes.
- You do not need the capabilities of the destination application to make changes.
- You have access to the source application *and* the source document.

To set up a link between an *Excel* worksheet range and a *Word* document:

- In *Excel*, select the worksheet range you want to link to the *Word* document.
- Click on the **COPY** button on the *Excel* toolbar.
- Switch to *Word.*
- Choose **EDIT/Paste Special** at the *Word* menu.
- Click on **Paste Link**.

- Select the format in which you want to insert the data in *Word.*
- Click on **OK** or press **ENTER**.

To View the Code for the Link:

- Select the linked object.
- Press **SHIFT+F9**.
- To return to the display of the object, press **SHIFT+F9** again.

Activity 3.1: Linking an Excel Worksheet Range and Chart to a Word Document

In this activity you will link first an *Excel* worksheet range and then an *Excel* chart to a *Word* document.

1. Start Microsoft Office. Use the *Microsoft Office* toolbar to open *Word.*
2. Insert your data disk and open the document called **sources.doc**.

   This document is a memo from the treasurer of the Powell Community Orchestra to the members of the Finance Committee.

3. Read the memo.
4. Switch to *Excel.*
5. Open the file **inc91-94.xls**.
6. Select the range **A1:E8**.
7. Choose **EDIT/Copy** or click on the **COPY** button on the *Excel* toolbar.
8. Switch to *Word.*
9. Use **CTRL+END** to go to the end of the document. The insertion point should be two lines below the end of the text.
10. At the *Word* menu bar, choose **EDIT/Paste Special**.
11. Click on the **Paste Link** option button.

    Notice that the option ***Formatted Text (RTF)*** *has been selected. This means that the worksheet range will be added to the Word document as a Word table. This is* ***not*** *the choice to make — editing the file in Word will defeat your purpose, which is to edit the Source, not the Destination document. Do* ***not*** *choose* ***Formatted Text (RTF)*** *when you link an Excel object with a Word document!*

12. Click on the line reading **Microsoft Excel 5.0 Worksheet Object** (Figure 3 -2).
13. Click on **OK** or press **ENTER**.
14. Notice that the linked worksheet range is now part of the *Word* document. To see the code for the link, click on the worksheet to select it and press **SHIFT+F9** (Figure 3 - 3).
15. Read the code.

    Notice that it specifies the location of the source and the range of the worksheet link.

16. Press **SHIFT+F9** to see the linked object again.
17. Return to the *Excel* worksheet.

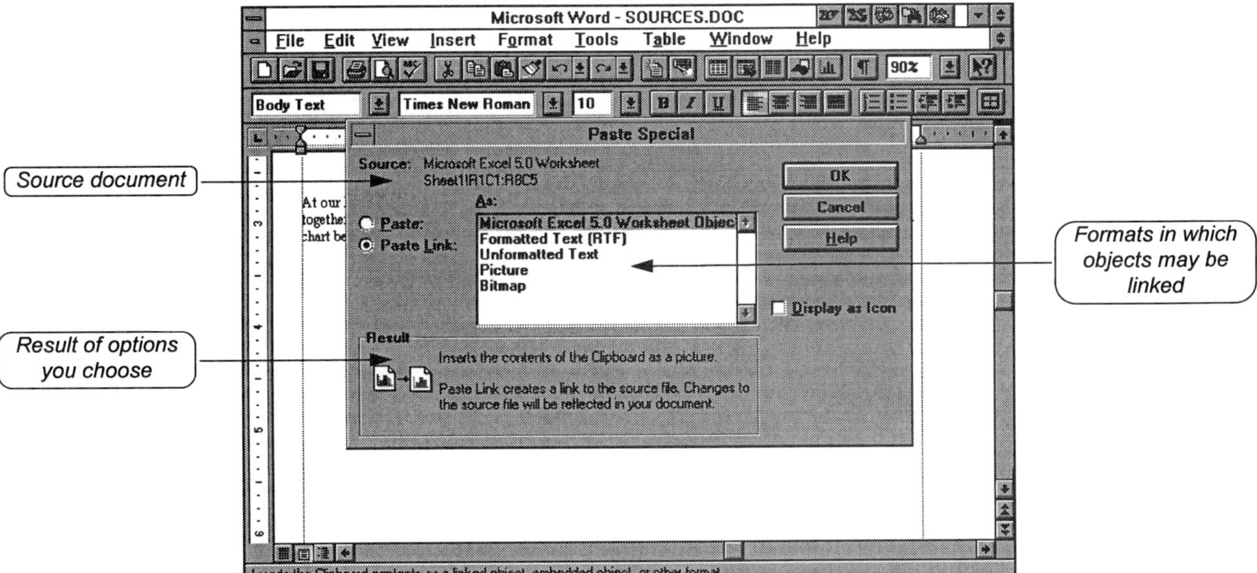

Figure 3 - 2 Linking an Excel Worksheet Object to Word

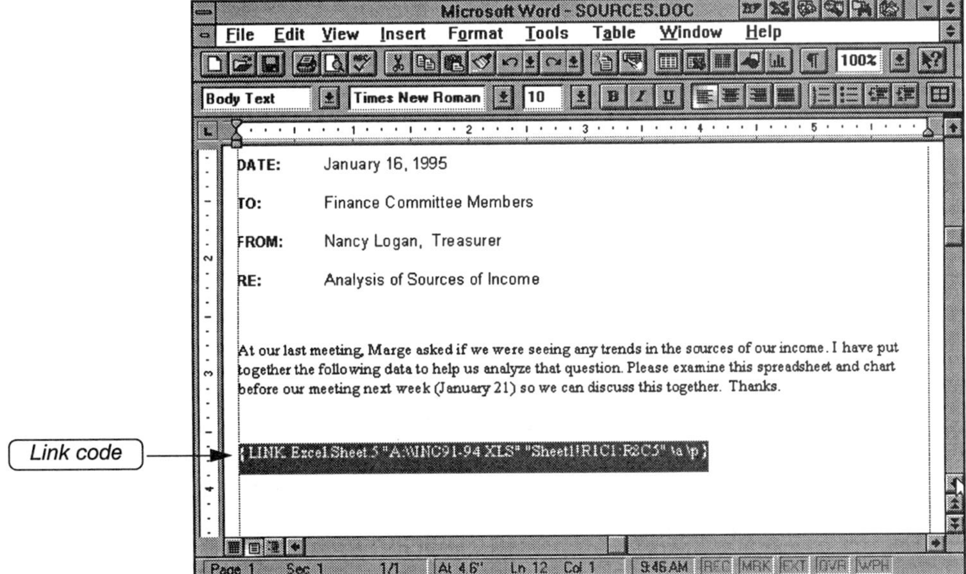

Figure 3 - 3 The code for the linked worksheet object

18. Examine the chart below the worksheet.

    Notice how the chart graphs the worksheet data.

19. Click on the chart once to select it.
20. Click on the **COPY** button on the *Excel* toolbar.
21. Switch to **sources.doc** in *Word.*
22. Click just past the worksheet and press **ENTER** twice.
23. At the *Word* menu, choose **EDIT/Paste Special**.

    Notice this time that there are only two choices on the menu, linking the chart as a ***Microsoft Excel 5.0 Chart Object*** *or as a* ***Picture****.*

24. Click on the **Paste Link** button (Figure 3 - 4).

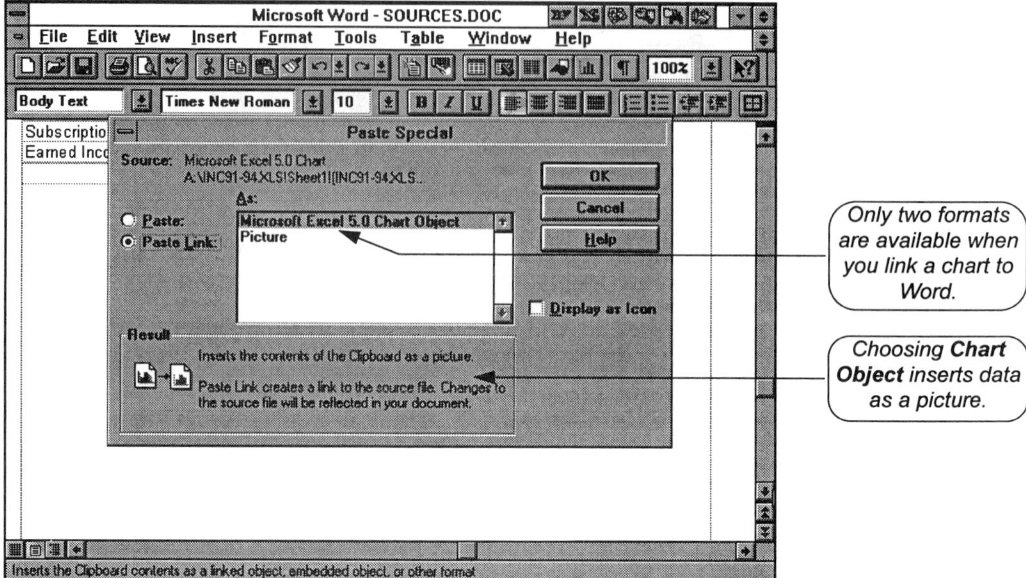

Figure 3 - 4 Linking a chart as an Excel 5.0 Chart Object to Word

25. Choose **Microsoft Excel 5.0 Chart Object**.

    *In this case there is absolutely **no** difference between choosing **Chart Object** and choosing **Picture.** Either choice inserts the contents of the Clipboard as a picture. In general, there are fewer choices of how to paste data when linking than when embedding, since all editing of linked objects is done at the source document.*

26. Click on **OK** or press **ENTER**.
27. Click on one of the objects (the worksheet or the chart).

    As we learned with embedded objects, when a linked object is selected it can be resized or moved. You will center the objects.

28. Center it by clicking the **CENTER** button on the **Formatting** toolbar. Select and center the second object.
29. **Save** your *Word* file **as sources1.doc**. Your document will resemble Figure 3 -5. Leave your files open for the next activity.

NOTE: *While changing the name of the Source document can break the link, changing the name of the Destination document has no effect.*

EDITING LINKED OBJECTS

When we discuss editing linked objects we are talking about changing the *contents* of the linked objects. This is done by editing the source document. The source document may be reached by opening it directly or by double-clicking on the linked object (in the destination document).

It is important to understand the distinction between editing a linked object and editing an embedded object. When you edit a linked object, *all* changes must be made to the source document, because that is the only accurate way to update both parts of the link.

As you learned in Lesson 2, when you edit an embedded object you must always remember that you have not returned to the source *document* — you have only returned to the source *application.* You use the source application to edit the embedded object, which is only a copy of the source document.

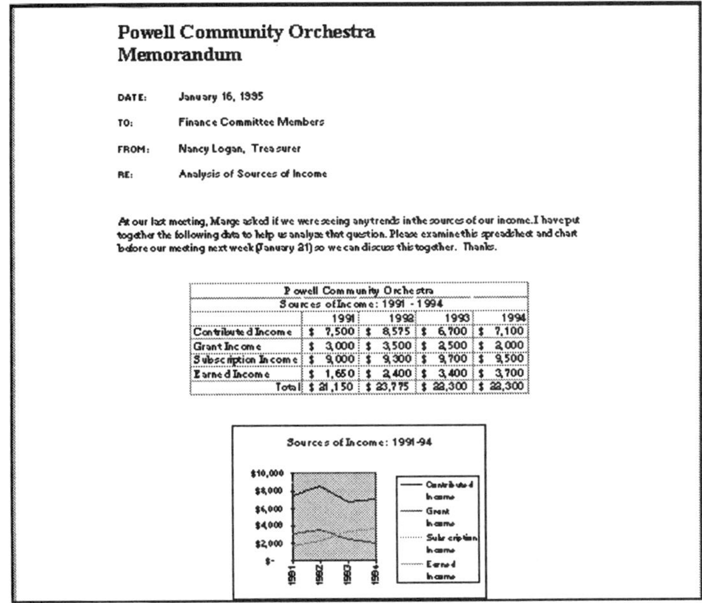

Powell Community Orchestra
Memorandum

DATE: January 16, 1995

TO: Finance Committee Members

FROM: Nancy Logan, Treasurer

RE: Analysis of Sources of Income

At our last meeting, Marge asked if we were seeing any trends in the sources of our income. I have put together the following data to help us analyze that question. Please examine this spreadsheet and chart before our meeting next week (January 21) so we can discuss this together. Thanks.

Powell Community Orchestra				
Sources of Income: 1991 - 1994				
	1991	1992	1993	1994
Contributed Income	$ 7,500	$ 8,575	$ 6,700	$ 7,100
Grant Income	$ 3,000	$ 3,500	$ 2,500	$ 2,000
Subscription Income	$ 9,000	$ 9,300	$ 9,700	$ 9,500
Earned Income	$ 1,650	$ 2,400	$ 3,400	$ 3,700
Total	$ 21,150	$ 23,775	$ 22,300	$ 22,300

Sources of Income: 1991-94

Figure 3 - 5 The memo sources1.doc after Activity 3.1

One of the reasons that the differences between editing linked and embedded objects are difficult to remember is because the instructions on the Status Bar (**Double-click to edit**...,) are the same for both procedures, whether the object is linked or embedded (Figure 3 - 6). When you double-click on an embedded object, you return to the source application but not the source document. ***When you double-click on a linked object, you return to the source document itself!***

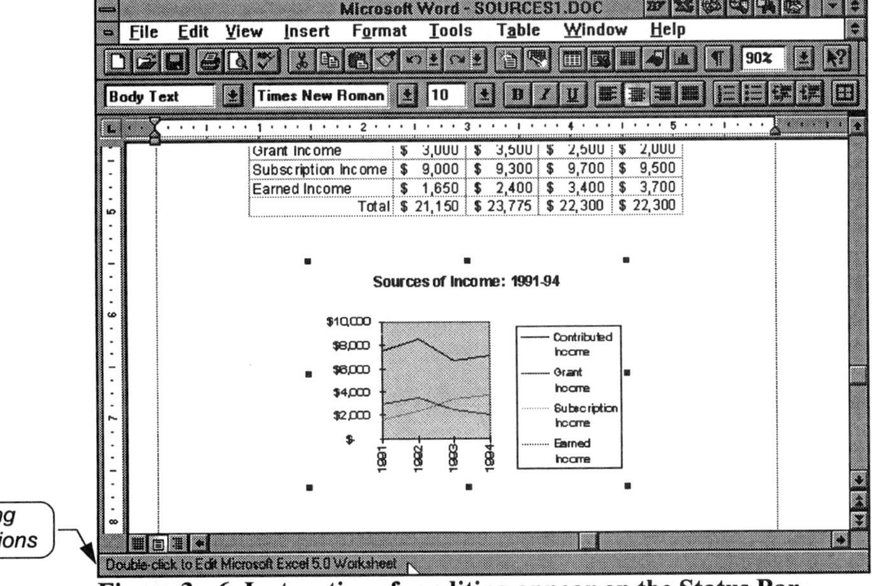

Figure 3 - 6 Instructions for editing appear on the Status Bar

CAUTION: *If you have linked a worksheet object as **Formatted** or **Unformatted** text, Word will appear to let you edit the object as if it were a Word table. However, since you are not following the rule of editing the source document, any editing changes you make to the destination document will disappear when the links are updated. Remember **not** to link worksheet data as **Formatted** or **Unformatted** text.*

To edit a linked object:

- Be sure that both the source and destination documents and applications are available.
- Open the source document.
- Or, if you are working in the destination document, select the object to be edited and double-click to return to the source for editing.
- Make the editing changes.
- Save the source document, using the *same* name.

  *The editing changes should also be reflected in the destination document, unless the **Automatic** Update setting has been changed to **Manual**. You will learn more about updating links later in this lesson.*

Activity 3.2: Changing the Linked Data

You have received new information about the orchestra's 1994 income. In this activity, you will make corrections to the source data. The changes will be automatically updated in the linked destination document.

1. Open *Excel* and open the source document **inc91-94.xls**.

   *The destination document in Word, **sources1.doc**, must be available, but does not need to be open.*

2. Make cell **E4** the active cell.

   A contribution of $500 has been credited to 1994 income.

3. Change the cell value to **7600**.

   If you are working on a network, or if you have a slow computer, this may take a long time. You will know that the change is recorded when the 7600 picks up the currency formatting of the other cells.

4. Scroll down in the worksheet and you will see that the chart has been changed as well (Figure 3 - 7).

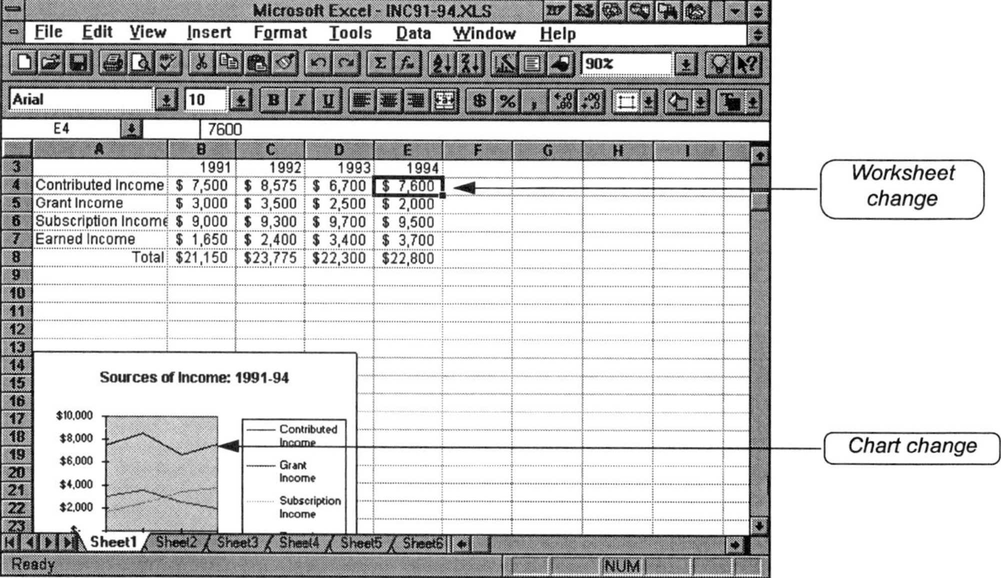

Figure 3 - 7 The source object has been edited

5. Switch to *Word* and look at **sources1.doc**.

   In most cases, you will see that both the worksheet and the chart reflect the editing change you made to the source (Figure 3 - 8).

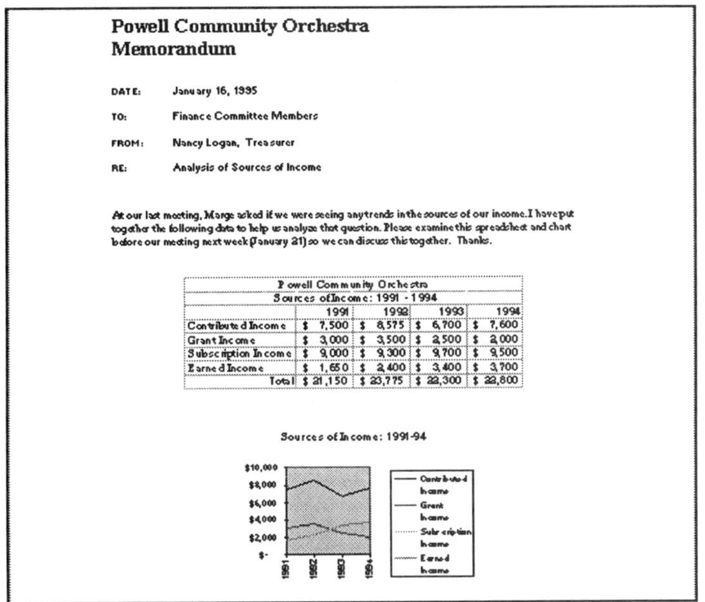

Powell Community Orchestra
Memorandum

DATE: January 16, 1995

TO: Finance Committee Members

FROM: Nancy Logan, Treasurer

RE: Analysis of Sources of Income

At our last meeting, Marge asked if we were seeing any trends in the sources of our income. I have put together the following data to help us analyze that question. Please examine this spreadsheet and chart before our meeting next week (January 21) so we can discuss this together. Thanks.

Powell Community Orchestra				
Sources of Income: 1991 - 1994				
	1991	1992	1993	1994
Contributed Income	$ 7,500	$ 8,575	$ 6,700	$ 7,600
Grant Income	$ 3,000	$ 3,500	$ 2,500	$ 2,000
Subscription Income	$ 9,000	$ 9,300	$ 9,700	$ 9,500
Earned Income	$ 1,650	$ 2,400	$ 3,400	$ 3,700
Total	$ 21,150	$ 23,775	$ 22,300	$ 22,800

Figure 3 - 8 Editing changes updated in destination document

PROBLEM SOLVER: *Make sure that you have not forgotten to save your file (Activity 3.1, Step 29). If the link still does not update, at the Word menu bar choose* ***EDIT/Links****. Click on each link individually, check that* ***Automatic*** *is selected at the bottom of the box, and click on* ***Update Now****. When finished, click on* ***Close****.*

6. Return to *Excel.*
7. Make cell **E7** the active cell.

   An additional $50 must be credited.

8. Change the cell value to **3750**.
9. Check that the change is reflected in the chart below.
10. Switch to *Word* and check that the change is displayed in both the worksheet and chart.

    If not, follow the ***Problem Solver*** *is Step 5.*

11. Save the file as **sources2.doc**. Your document will resemble Figure 3 -9.
12. Leave both files and applications open for the next activity.

Updating Links

Every document that contains linked objects contains a dialog box in which the links are listed and described. If a link is not functioning properly, this box should be opened and examined for errors. To reach the box, choose **EDIT/Links** at the menu bar of the document containing the link.

The information about each link is displayed in the **Links** dialog box as seen in Table 3 - 1.

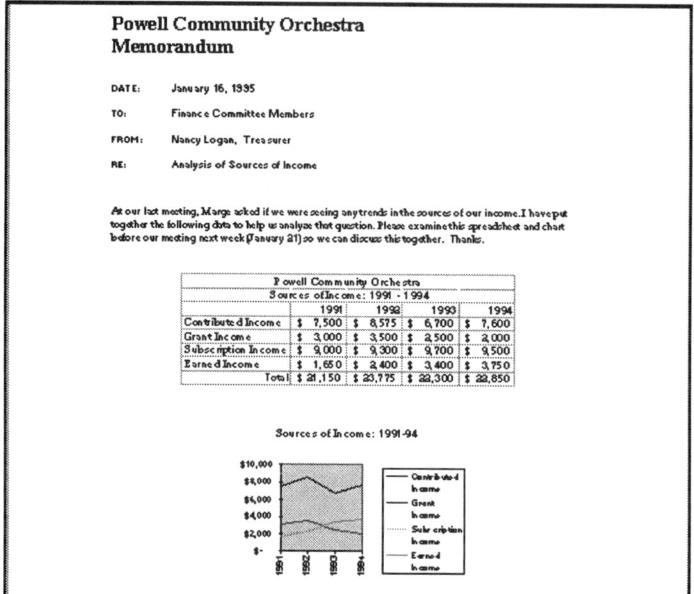

Powell Community Orchestra
Memorandum

DATE: January 16, 1995

TO: Finance Committee Members

FROM: Nancy Logan, Treasurer

RE: Analysis of Sources of Income

At our last meeting, Marge asked if we were seeing any trends in the sources of our income. I have put together the following data to help us analyze that question. Please examine this spreadsheet and chart before our meeting next week (January 21) so we can discuss this together. Thanks.

Powell Community Orchestra				
Sources of Income: 1991 - 1994				
	1991	1992	1993	1994
Contributed Income	$ 7,500	$ 8,575	$ 6,700	$ 7,600
Grant Income	$ 3,000	$ 3,500	$ 2,500	$ 2,000
Subscription Income	$ 9,000	$ 9,300	$ 9,700	$ 9,500
Earned Income	$ 1,650	$ 2,400	$ 3,400	$ 3,750
Total	$ 21,150	$ 23,775	$ 22,300	$ 22,850

Figure 3 - 9 The memo sources2.doc after Activity 3.2

Source File	The name of the file which contains the source of the linked data
Item	The name of the link, describing the exact location of the linked data
Type	The type of object that has been linked
Update	The manner in which changes to the source are updated to the linked file

Table 3 - 1: Information in the Links dialog box

Updating links refers to how the destination files are updated when the source data is changed. Links may be updated *automatically*, which means that the destination file will be updated without you having to take any additional action. Links may also be updated *manually*, which means that you perform the update by clicking the **Update Now** button in the **Links** dialog box. By default, links are set to update automatically. If you prefer not to use the automatic update, choose the **Manual** button at the **Links** dialog box.

If you have chosen the **Manual** update of linked documents, as long as the source document has been saved you may perform the update at any time you wish. If you have chosen **Locked**, the link is closed, and may not be updated. To update a link that is locked, change the type of update to **Automatic** or **Manual**.

To update links:

- If the **Links** dialog box is set to **Automatic**, there is usually no need to take any action. The destination file will be automatically updated when the source file is edited. If this does not occur, something is probably wrong with the link (see **Breaking and Modifying Links**).
- If the **Links** dialog box is set to **Manual**, open the box and click on the button marked **Update Now**. Click on **Close**.
- If the **Links** dialog box is set to **Locked**, open the box, unlock the link by clicking the **Manual** button, click on the button marked **Update Now**, and click on **OK**. If you wish, you may reset the link to **Locked**.

NOTE: *If your destination document is closed when you are changing the source, this will prevent it from being updated. In this case the update will be performed the next time you open the destination document. When you open a destination document that is due for an update, the message:* ***Updating linked files*** *or the message* ***Word is updating the fields in this document*** *will appear on the Status Bar.*

Activity 3.3: Updating Links Manually

In the last activity, you saw how links are automatically updated after editing occurs. In this exercise you will update the link manually.

1. In *Word*, make **sources2.doc** the active document.
2. At the menu, choose **EDIT/Links**.
3. Select **each** link and click on the **Manual** button at the bottom of the box (Figure 3 - 10).

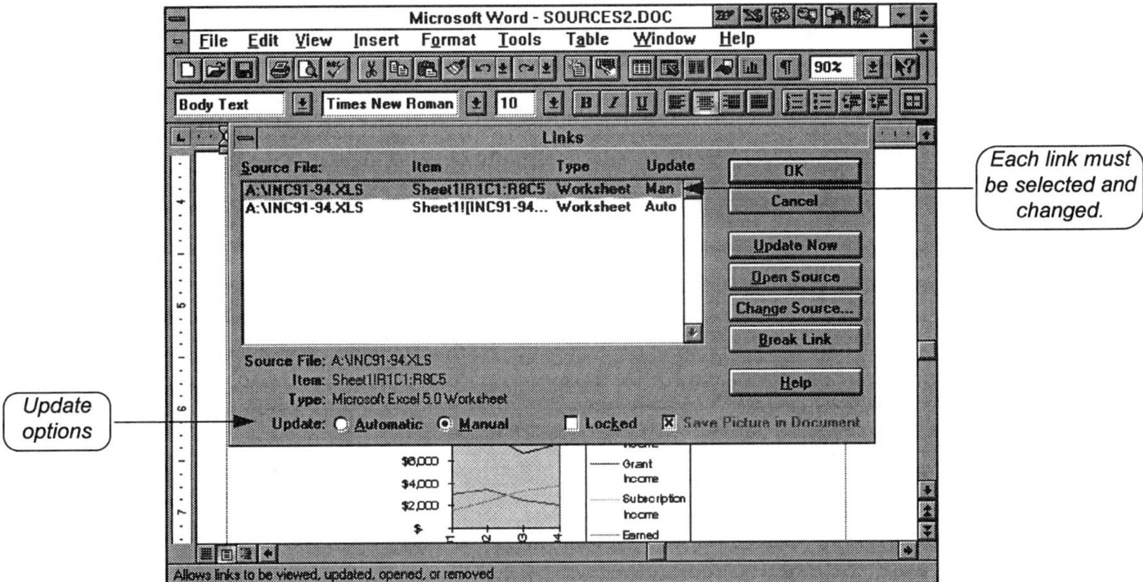

Figure 3 - 10 Changing to a Manual update of linked objects

4. Click on **OK** or press **ENTER**.
5. Switch to the *Excel* file **inc91-94.xls**.
6. Make cell **E5** the active cell.
7. Change the value to **1500**.

   Notice that the change is reflected in the chart below the worksheet.
8. Switch back to **sources2.doc** in *Word.*

   This time you will notice that the file has not been updated.
9. At the menu, choose **EDIT/Links**.
10. At the right side of the dialog box, click on the button marked **Update Now** (Figure 3 - 11).
11. When the hourglass disappears, click on **Close**.

    Now you will see that the update has occurred and that you have controlled its timing with the ***Update Now*** *button.*

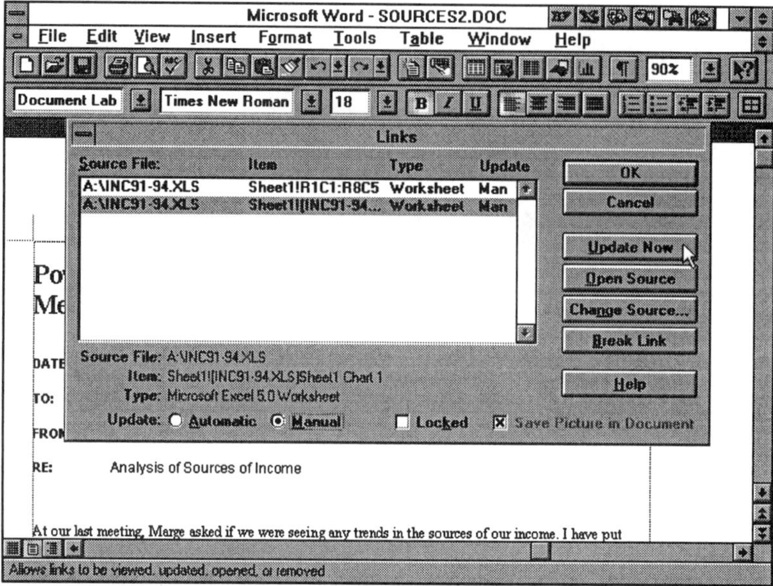

Figure 3 - 11 Updating links manually

12. Open the **EDIT/Links** box again.
13. Click on **each** link and choose the **Automatic** option.

    By doing this we are returning to the default setting.
14. Click on **OK** or press **ENTER**.
15. Save the *Word* file as **sources3.doc**. Your document will resemble Figure 3 - 12.

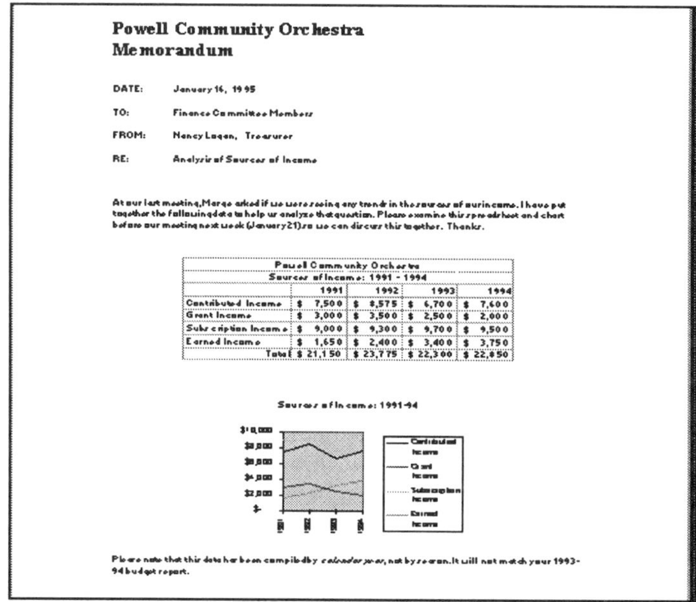

Powell Community Orchestra
Memorandum

DATE: January 16, 1995

TO: Finance Committee Members

FROM: Nancy Logan, Treasurer

RE: Analysis of Sources of Income

At our last meeting, Marge asked if we were seeing any trends in the sources of our income. I have put together the following data to help us analyze that question. Please examine this spreadsheet and chart before our meeting next week (January 21) so we can discuss this together. Thanks.

Powell Community Orchestra				
Sources of Income: 1991 - 1994				
	1991	1992	1993	1994
Contributed Income	$ 7,500	$ 8,575	$ 6,700	$ 7,600
Grant Income	$ 3,000	$ 3,500	$ 2,500	$ 2,000
Subscription Income	$ 9,000	$ 9,300	$ 9,700	$ 9,500
Earned Income	$ 1,650	$ 2,400	$ 3,400	$ 3,750
Total	$ 21,150	$ 23,775	$ 22,300	$ 22,850

Sources of Income: 1991-94

Please note that this data has been compiled by calendar year, not by season. It will not match your 1993-94 budget report.

Figure 3 - 12 The memo sources3.doc after Activity 3.3

16. Switch to *Excel* and save **inc91-94.xls** without changing its name.
17. Leave the files open for the next activity.

Breaking and Modifying Links

Breaking a link means severing the connection between the two parts of the link — the source and destination documents. For a link to function properly, everything must be set just right. The source file, name, type, and update specification in the **Links** dialog box must be set correctly. Sometimes you will *want* to break a link so that no more updates are possible. You can do this by selecting the link and clicking the **Break Link** button.

Much of the time, when links do not work, they have been broken accidentally, and the user is unaware of what has happened. If your link is broken, the source data may not appear — or else the data will appear but will not update as the source is edited. Sometimes there will be an error message, sometimes not. But it is up to you to modify or fix the link.

Modifying a link means making changes to the link code so that it will work. Modifications to the link may be made at the **Links** dialog box, which contains buttons marked **Open Source, Change Source,** and **Break Link**, or at the link code itself, which may be displayed in the document by pressing **SHIFT+F9** while the linked object is selected.

A common cause of broken links occurs when the source file has been renamed or moved to a different drive or directory. When this occurs the **Links** dialog box is frequently *not* updated. When the incorrect filename appears the link will not work properly. To fix the link, you must update the source filename in the **Links** dialog box or in the link code.

CAUTION: *Object Linking and Embedding (OLE) is still a new feature in Windows applications, and will not always perform as expected. The amount of RAM in your computer, the size of your file, the specific applications you are using, and network settings are only a few of many variables leading to inconsistent results.*

To break a link or modify a broken link:

- To break a link, open the **Links** dialog box, select the link you want to break, and click on the button marked **Break Link**.

  This should only be done when you will not want to update the link again.

- To modify a link, examine the **Links** dialog box, select the link that needs to be modified, and detect the error in the link specifications. If the source filename is incorrect, click on **Change Source**, select the correct filename and click on **OK**.
- If changing the dialog box does not repair the link, click on the object in the destination document, press **SHIFT+F9** to display the link code, and manually edit the link. Press **SHIFT+F9** again to display the object.
- If all else fails, and you cannot fix the link, first break the link and then reestablish it. To do this, choose **Break Link** and then **Yes** at the **Links** dialog box. Then, reestablish the link as you did in Activity 3.1.

Activity 3.4: Modifying a Link (Optional)

In the following activity, you will rename your source file, **inc91-94.xls**. This should break the links you have established. Then, you will repair, or modify those links, following instructions that should work. We have also included a second way to modify the links, if the first method fails. This activity is optional, because Microsoft Office does not yet support these procedures reliably. You will practice these methods, and see how to fix links you accidentally break, but each time you try this exercise you may achieve different results. According to Microsoft Product Support Services, they are researching and correcting these problems, so the later the date of your release of Microsoft Office, the better your chances of success in modifying links.

1. Close the *Excel* source file you have been working with, **inc91-94.xls**.

   *If you are asked if you want to save files, choose **Yes**.*

2. Open the Windows File Manager.

HINT: *Return to the Program Manager, open the Main program group, and double-click on the File Manager icon.*

3. Display the files on your data disk.
4. In the **File List**, click on **inc91-94.xls** (Figure 3 -13).

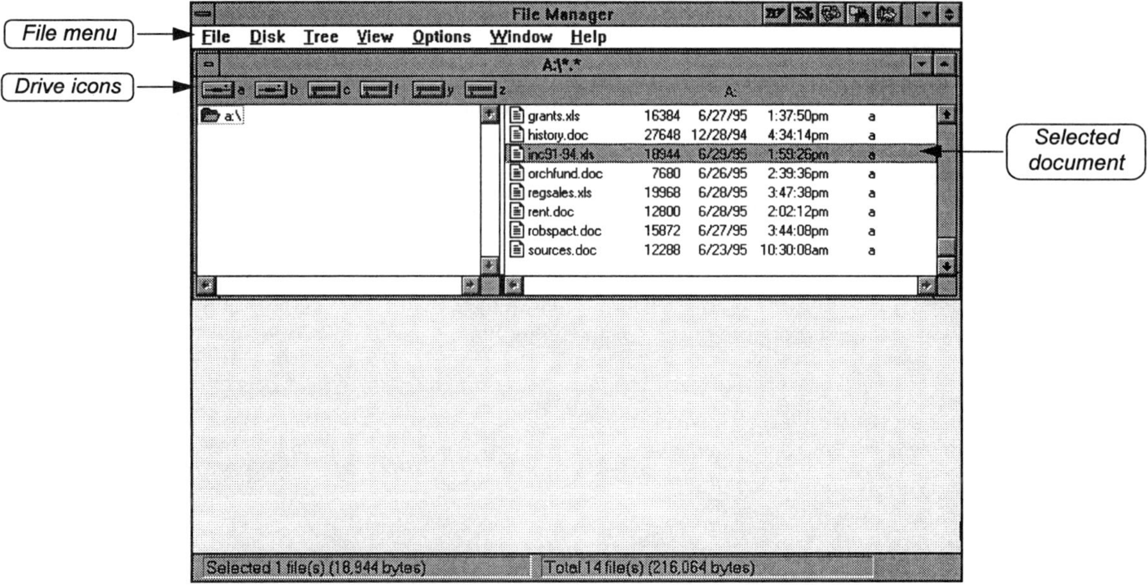

Figure 3 - 13 Locating the current source file in the File Manager

5. At the menu, choose **FILE/Rename**.
6. Rename the file **changed.xls**, and click on **OK** (Figure 3 -14).

*Be sure you type the full filename, including the **.xls** extension, or you will not see the file listing when you return to Excel.*

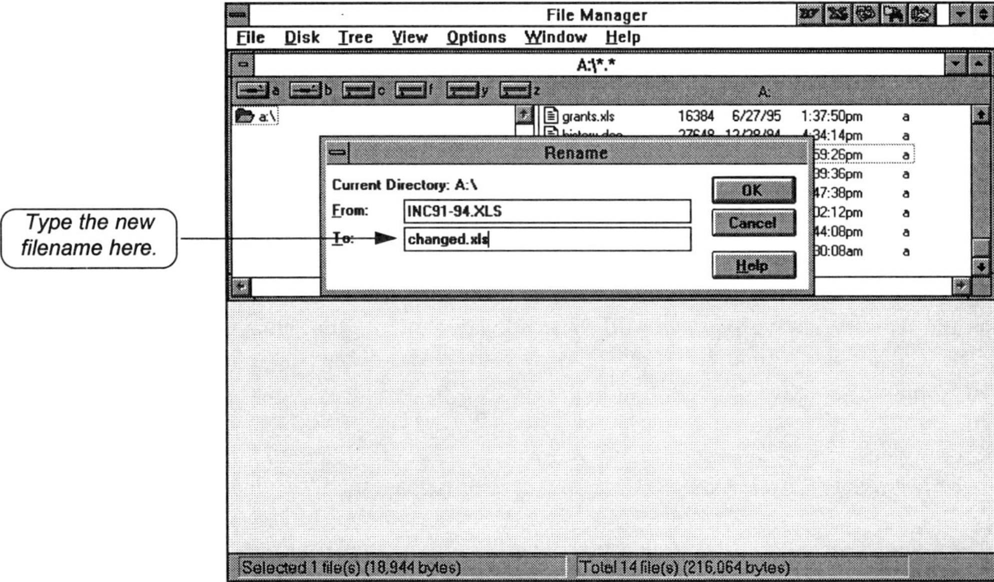

Figure 3 - 14 Renaming the source file

7. Return to *Excel*, leaving the File Manager open, in case you need to repeat the exercise.

NOTE: *If you rename the file using **FILE/Save As** you may see the source filename automatically updated. Instead, we have used the File Manager to rename the file so that you will have the experience of trying various ways to modify the link.*

8. Switch to *Word* and the destination document, **sources3.doc**.
9. At the menu, choose **EDIT/Links**.
   a) If the source filename reads **changed.xls,** the new source filename, you will not need to modify the links and you may skip to **Step 20**.
   b) If the source filename still reads **inc91-94.xls**, the old source filename, you will need to change the source filename. To do this, continue with **Step 10**.
10. At the **EDIT/Links** box, with the first link selected, click on the **Change Source** button.
11. Choose the new file name, **changed.xls**, and click on **OK** (Figure 3 - 15).

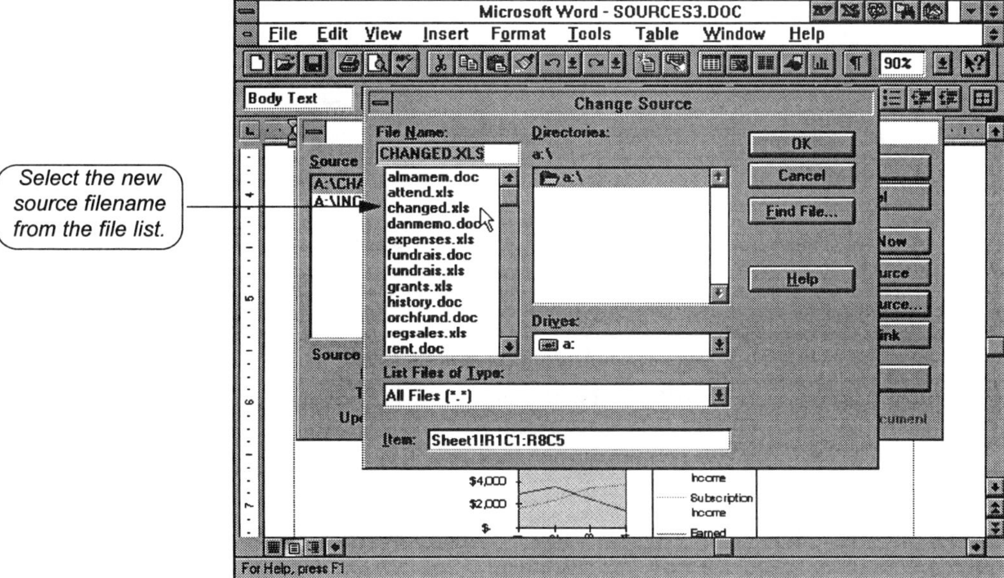

Figure 3 - 15 Changing the link code for the Source File

12. Repeat Steps 10 and 11 for the second link.
    a) If the links now specify **changed.xls**, choose **OK** to leave the **Links** dialog box. Then open the dialog box again. If the filename still specifies **changed.xls**, you have been successful in modifying the link. You may proceed with **Step 20**.
    b) If, after re-opening the **Links** dialog box, the filename has reverted back to **inc91-94.xls**, the link has not been modified. You will try another method to modify the link by continuing with **Step 13.**
    c) If the link never changed at all when you used the **Change Source** command, you must try another method to modify the link. Proceed with **Step 13**.
13. Close the **Edit Links** dialog box.
14. At the **sources3.doc** screen, click on the worksheet or chart.
15. Press **SHIFT+F9** to display the full code for the links.
16. Click on the worksheet code, and use normal editing procedures to get the filename to read **changed.xls**.

17. Click on the chart code and make the same change ***twice*** because the filename is mentioned two times (Figure 3 -16).

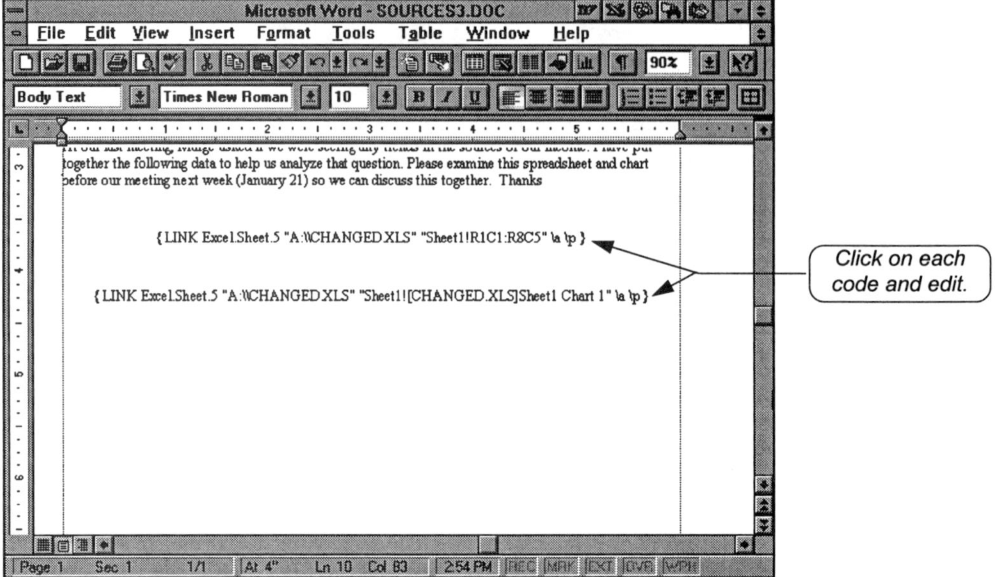

Figure 3 - 16 Editing the link codes in the destination document

18. Press **SHIFT+F9** again to display the objects instead of the link codes.
19. Check the **Links** dialog box and you should see that your changes have taken effect.
    a) If you have succeeded in modifying your links, we will test them with the next few steps.
    b) **LAST RESORT:** If the links still have not been modified, you may re-do them by selecting and deleting each object from your destination document, and then re-linking them from the source document (now **changed.xls**). If you need help, consult Activity 3.1. After you have re-done the links, continue with **Step 20**.
20. To test the repaired link, double-click on the worksheet to return to **changed.xls**.
21. Make cell **E6** active and change the value to **9900**.
22. Return to **sources3.doc** and check to see that your file has been updated, proving that the link has been re-established effectively.

    You may need to update the links manually.
23. Position your cursor below the chart, change back to Left Alignment, and add the following text to the end of the memo:

    Please note that this data has been compiled by *calendar year,* not by season. It will not match your 1993-94 budget report.
24. Check the spelling of the document.
25. **Save** the destination file **as sources4.doc**. Your document will resemble Figure 3 - 17.
26. Print the file.
27. Save the source file, keeping the same name.
28. Print the source file.
29. Close both the source and destination files.
30. Exit from *Word* and *Excel.*

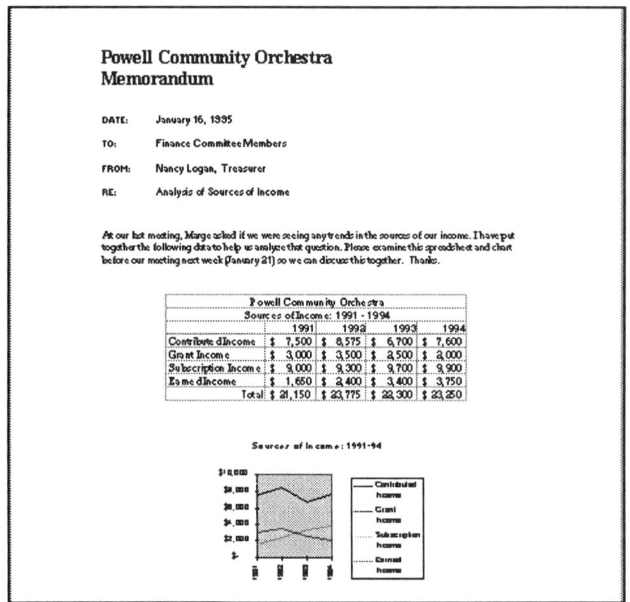

Powell Community Orchestra
Memorandum

DATE: January 16, 1995

TO: Finance Committee Members

FROM: Nancy Logan, Treasurer

RE: Analysis of Sources of Income

At our last meeting, Marge asked if we were seeing any trends in the sources of our income. I have put together the following data to help us analyze that question. Please examine this spreadsheet and chart before our meeting next week (January 21) so we can discuss this together. Thanks.

Powell Community Orchestra				
Sources of Income: 1991 - 1994				
	1991	1992	1993	1994
Contributed Income	$ 7,500	$ 8,575	$ 6,700	$ 7,600
Grant Income	$ 3,000	$ 3,500	$ 2,500	$ 2,000
Subscription Income	$ 9,000	$ 9,300	$ 9,700	$ 9,900
Earned Income	$ 1,650	$ 2,400	$ 3,400	$ 3,750
Total	$ 21,150	$ 23,775	$ 22,300	$ 23,250

Figure 3 - 17 The memo sources4.doc after Activity 3.4

SUMMARY

The main difference between embedding and linking is that linked objects remain connected to each other — you edit the source and destination objects in one operation.

Differences between Embedding and Linking Objects:

Embedded Object	Linked Object
• Increase in file size is much larger than that accounted for by the formatted text; the entire source file and all of the information needed to edit the object in the source application are stored in the destination file.	• Increase in file size is much less than in embedded object. The object data is not physically placed within the destination file.
• The destination object is edited using the commands of the source application. The source is not changed.	• Only the source object is edited. The destination object is updated when or after the source is edited.
• The source document is never used after it is embedded, so it need not be available.	• The source document must be available or the linked object cannot be seen in the destination document.
• The source application must be on the computer in order to edit the object.	• The source application *and the source document* must be on the computer in order to edit the linked object.
• It is easy to transport the file from computer to computer unless the file size is larger than the floppy disk capacity.	• It is difficult to transport the file to a different computer. The destination and all source files must be moved, and the source files must have the same location (drive and directory) as in the original computer.

Similarities between Embedding and Linking Objects:

- You use the **Copy** and **Paste Special** functions for both.
- You will see the instruction: **Double-click to edit object** on the Status Bar for both.
- All aspects of the source object (text, formatting, formulas) are present in the destination object.

KEY TERMS

Automatic Update	Link Code	Rename
Break Link	Links Dialog Box	Source File
Change Source	Locked link	Update Now
Item	Manual Update	
Link	Open Source	

INDEPENDENT PROJECTS

Independent Project 3.1: Linking a Worksheet with a Document

In this project, you are a talent agent, working for a rock band called **Olde English**. The band makes frequent appearances at college campuses, usually in or near the Eastern part of the country. You will be linking and updating a worksheet object summarizing the bookings for next season with a memo sent to the band manager, band members and others, keeping them informed of additions and changes to the schedule.

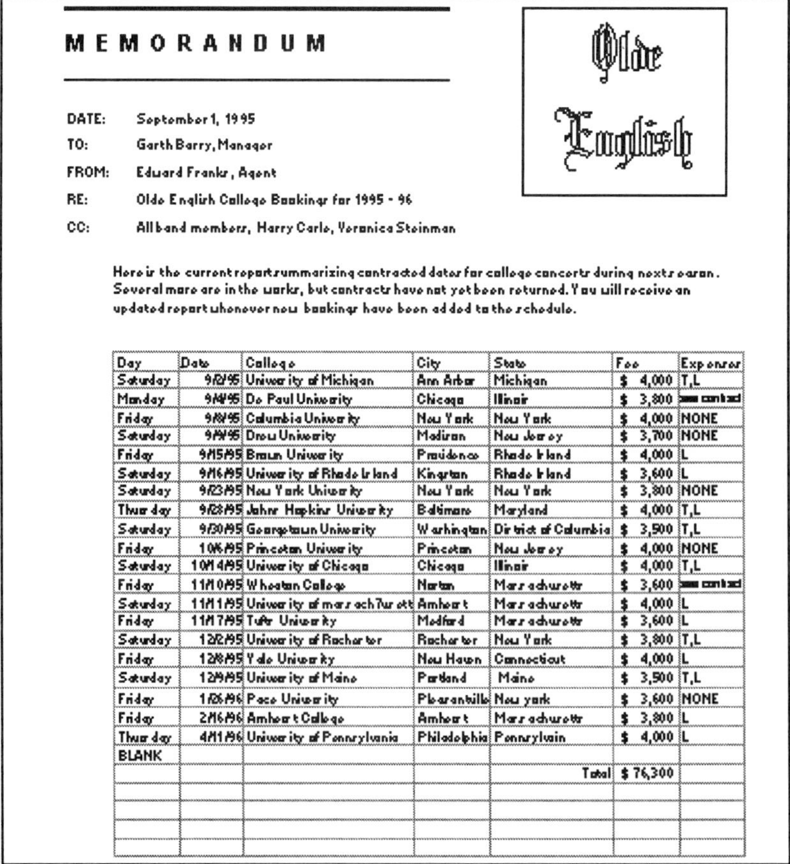

M E M O R A N D U M

Olde English

DATE: September 1, 1995

TO: Garth Barry, Manager

FROM: Edward Franks, Agent

RE: Olde English College Bookings for 1995 - 96

CC: All band members, Harry Carle, Veronica Steinman

Here is the current report summarizing contracted dates for college concerts during next season. Several more are in the works, but contracts have not yet been returned. You will receive an updated report whenever new bookings have been added to the schedule.

Day	Date	College	City	State	Fee	Expenses
Saturday	9/2/95	University of Michigan	Ann Arbor	Michigan	$ 4,000	T,L
Monday	9/4/95	De Paul University	Chicago	Illinois	$ 3,800	[illegible] contract
Friday	9/8/95	Columbia University	New York	New York	$ 4,000	NONE
Saturday	9/9/95	Drew University	Madison	New Jersey	$ 3,700	NONE
Friday	9/15/95	Brown University	Providence	Rhode Island	$ 4,000	L
Saturday	9/16/95	University of Rhode Island	Kingston	Rhode Island	$ 3,600	L
Saturday	9/23/95	New York University	New York	New York	$ 3,800	NONE
Thursday	9/28/95	Johns Hopkins University	Baltimore	Maryland	$ 4,000	T,L
Saturday	9/30/95	Georgetown University	Washington	District of Columbia	$ 3,500	T,L
Friday	10/6/95	Princeton University	Princeton	New Jersey	$ 4,000	NONE
Saturday	10/14/95	University of Chicago	Chicago	Illinois	$ 4,000	T,L
Friday	11/10/95	Wheaton College	Norton	Massachusetts	$ 3,600	[illegible] contract
Saturday	11/11/95	University of massach7usett	Amherst	Massachusetts	$ 4,000	L
Friday	11/17/95	Tufts University	Medford	Massachusetts	$ 3,600	L
Saturday	12/2/95	University of Rochester	Rochester	New York	$ 3,800	T,L
Friday	12/8/95	Yale University	New Haven	Connecticut	$ 4,000	L
Saturday	12/9/95	University of Maine	Portland	Maine	$ 3,500	T,L
Friday	1/26/96	Pace University	Pleasantville	New york	$ 3,600	NONE
Friday	2/16/96	Amherst College	Amherst	Massachusetts	$ 3,800	L
Thursday	4/11/96	University of Pennsylvania	Philadelphia	Pennsylvain	$ 4,000	L
BLANK						
				Total	$ 76,300	

Figure 3 - 18: Completed version of the document

1. Open Microsoft Office and *Word.*
2. From your data disk, open the document called **bookings.doc**.
3. Read the memo, so that you will understand the project.
4. Press **CTRL+END** to reach the end of the document.

   Your cursor should be positioned two lines below the paragraph of text.
5. Open *Excel* and the worksheet **bookings.xls**.
6. Examine the worksheet, noting the column headings and current bookings.
7. Select the range **A4:G4** (the column headings) and make it bold.
8. Select **A1:G2** and center the text across columns.
9. Leaving the text selected, make it bold.
10. Resave the worksheet, keeping the same name.
11. Select **A4:G30**. Notice the word **BLANK** in **A20**.

    You are selecting extra rows so that you will have room to add new data to the worksheet. If you run out of empty rows as you add to the memo, you will have to delete the linked object, and set up a new link. We will also keep the row ***above*** *the total blank. Keeping this row blank and within the range included in the sum allows the* ***Sum*** *function to operate correctly as we add rows to the worksheet.*
12. Choose **EDIT/Copy**, or click on the **COPY** button on the toolbar.
13. Switch to *Word.*
14. Choose **EDIT/Paste Special**, and **Paste Link** the worksheet as either a **Microsoft Excel 5.0 Worksheet Object**, or as a **Picture**. There is no difference between these choices in this situation.

PROBLEM SOLVER: *If the worksheet object does not fit within the margins, keep it selected and choose* ***FORMAT/Paragraph****. Change the* ***Left Indent*** *to* ***0*** *and choose* ***OK****.*

15. Keep the object you just linked selected and choose **EDIT/Links** at the menu.
16. Make sure the **Update** is set to **Automatic.** Choose **OK**.
17. Save the file as **coltour.doc**.
18. Print the file.

    By the middle of August there have been several changes to the schedule. You will update the Excel worksheet, check that the linked memo has been updated, make other changes to the memo, and resave it.
19. Return to the *Excel* worksheet.
20. Press **ESC** to clear the paste message from the Status Bar and to remove the moving border around the copied range.
21. Select the entire row that contains **Tufts University** (row 17).
22. Choose **INSERT/Rows** to insert a blank row between **Wheaton College** and **Tufts University**.
23. Type the following data in cells **A17** through **G17**:

    Saturday 11/11/95 University of Massachusetts Amherst Massachusetts 4000 L
24. If the last cell (**G17**) is formatted in an 8 point font, change to **10** points.
25. Select rows **21** and **22**. Choose **INSERT/Rows** to insert two blank rows.

*Notice that the row containing the word **BLANK** and the row containing the **Total** are now rows **23** and **24**. As long as those rows are contingudus, the **Sum** will be accurate.*

26. Type the following data in the rows **21** and **22**.:

	A	*B*	*C*	*D*	*E*	*F*	*G*
21	**Saturda y**	**12/9/95**	**University of Maine**	**Portland**	**Maine**	**3500**	**T,L**
22	**Friday**	**1/26/96**	**Pace University**	**Pleasantville**	**New York**	**3600**	**NONE**

27. The **sum** function will have updated the total.
28. Save the *Excel* file, keeping the same name.
29. Switch to the *Word* memo, and check that the linked object has been updated properly.

HINT: *For help updating links, see Activity 3.3.*

30. Change the date on the memo to **August 15, 1995**.
31. Delete **Monica Rudes**, and add **Veronica Steinman**, to the **cc:** list.
32. Save the file as **coltour1.doc**.
33. Print the file.

By the beginning of September, you need to make more changes to the memo.

34. Switch to the *Excel* worksheet and select rows **23** and **24**.
35. Choose **INSERT/Rows** and type the following in rows 23 and 24:

	A	*B*	*C*	*D*	*E*	*F*	*G*
23	**Friday**	**2/16/96**	**Amherst College**	**Amherst**	**Massachusetts**	**3800**	**L**
24	**Thursday**	**4/11/96**	**University of Pennsylvania**	**Philadelphia**	**Pennsylvania**	**4000**	**L**

36. Again, the **sum** function will have updated the total.
37. Save the *Excel* file, keeping the same name.
38. Switch to the *Word* memo.
39. Check that the update has been performed properly.

If not, see the suggestions in Step 30.

40. Change the date of the memo to September 1, 1995.
41. Save the file as **coltour2.doc**. Your file should resemble Figure 3 - 18, pictured at the beginning of this project.

Independent Project 3.2: Linking Selected Items from Excel to a PowerPoint Presentation

The Chairperson of the Board of Trustees of the orchestra wants to use the presentation you created in Independent Project 1.2 for the various talks he gives about the orchestra throughout the year. He wants you to add two slides: a worksheet listing of the grants the orchestra has received, and a bar chart of this worksheet. Choosing the best way to insert the *Excel* worksheet data and chart into *PowerPoint* is not easy. Since the source data will be updated, we want the presentation to update also. Also, as you saw in Independent Project 2.2, when data from *Word* was *embedded* in *PowerPoint* the text color and size were not appropriate and had to be changed. Therefore, we have decided to link the information from *Excel,* and we have reached a compromise which allows the data to look good in both the *Excel* worksheet and the *PowerPoint* presentation. You will link the *Excel* worksheet data and the chart to the *PowerPoint* presentation, and you will format the data so that it is readable in *PowerPoint.* You will edit the data in the *Excel* worksheet and notice that the *PowerPoint* presentation is updated. When completed, slides 6 and 7 of your presentation will resemble Figures 3 - 19 and 3 - 20.

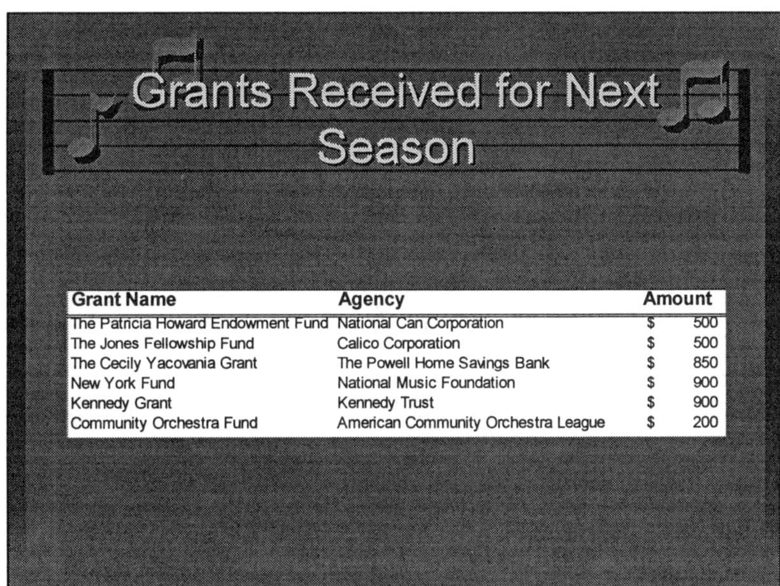

Figure 3 - 19: Completed Slide 6

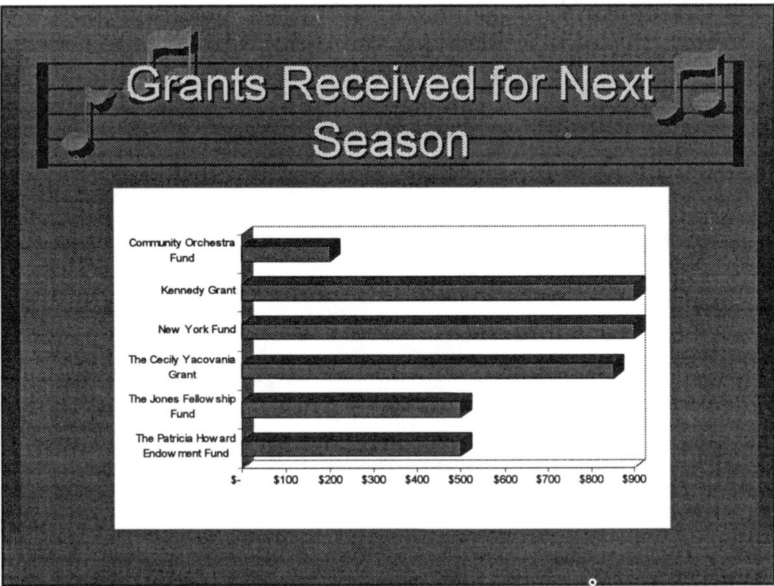

Figure 3 - 20: Completed Slide 7

1. Start Microsoft Office, if necessary. Use the Microsoft Office Toolbar to open *Excel.*
2. Open the **grants.xls** file.

   *The **grants.xls** file has a worksheet and a graph of grants received for next season.*
3. Highlight cells **A3:C9**.

4. Copy the selected range.
5. Use the *Microsoft Office* Toolbar to open *PowerPoint.*
6. Open the **history1.ppt** presentation.

   *If you have not done Independent Project 1.2, open **history.ppt**. There are the same number of slides in both presentations. **History.ppt** has only blank slides.*
7. Go to Slide 5 (the last slide in the presentation).
8. To add a slide to the presentation:
   - Click on the **New Slide** button on the Status bar.

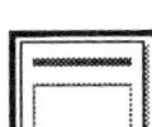

   - Scroll the list of **AutoLayouts**, and select the **Object** AutoLayout. Click on **OK**.
9. Click in the Title placeholder and type: **Grants Received for Next Season**
10. **DO NOT** double-click to add object (even though that is what is says onscreen). Instead, point to the border of the lower box and click on it once so that handles appear.
11. Use **EDIT/Paste Special** to **Paste Link** the **Microsoft Excel 5.0 Worsheet Object.**

    *The only choice available in the **As:** list box was **Microsoft Excel 5.0 Worksheet Object**.*

    The worksheet is placed on the slide with column and row lines showing, and the text is black. This color combination is difficult to read on the blue background. You will return to Excel and change the pattern of the background behind these cells to white. This will make the worksheet much easier to read in PowerPoint and still readable in Excel.
12. Double-click on the worksheet object to return to *Excel* to edit the source worksheet, **grants.xls.**

    Since you are editing the original worksheet, the range you copied should still be highlighted.
13. Choose **FORMAT/Cells.**
14. Choose the **Patterns** tab.

    *The **Sample** area is the same color as the background of the dialog box because no background color has been selected.*
15. Click on the ↓ in the **Pattern** drop-down list box.

    A pop-up dialog box appears with a palette of available colors and patterns.
16. Choose the plain white color (top row).
17. Click on **OK.**

    When you return to Excel, the background of the selected cells should be white. The background overlays the existing column and row lines.
18. Use the *Microsoft Office* toolbar to return to *PowerPoint.*

    The worksheet data now has a white background behind it and the black text is much easier to read.
19. Add another new slide as you did in Step 8, using the **Object** AutoLayout.
20. Add the following title:

    Grants Received for Next Season
21. Deselect the title by clicking on the border of the lower box so that handles appear..
22. Use the *Microsoft Office* toolbar to return to *Excel.*
23. Click once on the chart so that handles appear around the chart.

24. Copy the chart and **Paste Link** it into *PowerPoint.*

    The only choice that was available in the ***As:*** *list box was* ***Microsoft Excel 5.0 Chart Object****.*

    The Excel Object will be placed on the slide but once again some of the text is hard to read because it is black.

25. Double-click on the linked chart to switch back to *Excel* and edit **grants.xls**..
26. Double-click on the chart in *Excel.*
27. Select the **Plot** area by clicking on any of the blank space outside of the chart. (You will see the word **Plot** in the Name Box on the left-side of the Formula Bar.)
28. Click the right mouse button to bring up the short-cut menu.
29. Choose **Format Plot Area**.

    Notice that the sample area is once again the same color as the background of the dialog box.

30. Use the **Pattern** drop-down list box to change the background color to **white**.
31. Click on the *Excel* worksheet outside of the chart twice.
32. Return to *PowerPoint* and see how much clearer the chart looks.
33. **Save** the presentation **as: history2.ppt**
34. You have new information on the Kennedy Grant. Use the Office toolbar to return to *Excel.*
35. Change the amount of the Kennedy Grant to **900**.
36. Save the worksheet using the same name.
37. Exit *Excel.*

    You will return to your PowerPoint presentation. Check the Kennedy Grant information in both the worksheet and the graph. It both cases, it should be updated to show $900. Slides 6 and 7 should resemble Figures 3 - 19 and 3 - 20 (at the beginning of the project).

38. Save the presentation using the current name.
39. Print Slides 6 and 7 using the **Pure Black & White** option.
40. Close the **history2.ppt** presentation.
41. Exit *PowerPoint.*
42. Print the file.
43. Close both files and exit from Microsoft Office.

Independent Project 3.3: Linking a Word Document and an Excel Chart

The chairperson of the Powell Community Orchestra is working with a new organization which encourages people involved in community orchestras to share information. As part of a memo studying community orchestra budgeting, you have decided to include a pie chart of the Powell Community orchestra's expenditures for the last year. You are sending the memo out first in March, but will send it to other groups of people later. You always like to share accurate information, and you know that some of the expense items are not complete. Therefore, you are going to *link* the pie chart and the memo, so that future copies of the memo will have the latest expense breakdown. Your completed memo should resemble Figure 3 - 23.

1. Open Microsoft Office and *Word.*
2. Open **spend.doc**.
3. Read the memo.

4. Move the insertion point to the end of the document.
5. Open *Excel* and **expenses.xls**.
6. Choose the **1994-1995** sheet tab on the horizontal scroll bar if it is not already selected.
7. Select the expense categories and amounts in **A5:B17**.
8. Choose **INSERT/Chart,As New Sheet**.
9. Click on **Next** in the ChartWizard to reach the Step 2 of 5 dialog box.
10. Choose the **Pie** or **3-D Pie** chart and click on **Next**.
11. Choose format 7 on the next dialog box.
12. In the fifth dialog box, add a chart title of your choice. Click on **Finish**.
13. Select the chart by clicking in the white space outside of the pie. (When you do this, the name **Chart** should appear in the Name Box on the Formula Bar.)
14. Copy the chart and paste link it as a **Microsoft Excel 5.0 Chart Object** at the end of **spend.doc**.
15. If you think the pie chart is too big, click on it once to select it. Choose **FORMAT/Picture**. Change the **Scaling Width** and **Height** percentage to a smaller number. You can choose the number, just be sure to use the same percentage for the width and the height so that the chart will be scaled proportionally.
16. Center the chart.
17. **Save** the file **as**: **spend2**
18. Print the memo.
19. Switch to *Excel.*
20. Press **Esc** to remove the moving border from around the chart.
21. Choose the **1994-1995** tab.
22. Additional publicity and printing bills have arrived. Change the figure for publicity to **1000** and the printing costs to **3000**.
23. Save and close **expenses.xls** using the current name.
24. *Word* and **spend2.doc** should be on the screen. If they are not, switch to them.
25. Change the date of the memo to **May 1**.
26. In the second paragraph, at the end of the second sentence (*I am including a pie chart of the Powell Community Orchestra expenses for the past year*) add the following; **(updated to include the latest figures!)**
27. Save the file as **spend3.doc**.
28. Print the memo again. How much did the percent of the budget accounted for by publicity and by printing change?
29. Exit from *Word.*

Memorandum

DATE: May 1, 1995

TO: Members,
Community Orchestra Association

FROM: Ronald Borman, Chair
Board of Trustees
Powell Community Orchestra

RE: Budgeting Workshop Committee

Susan Ames from the Upper Newburgh Community Orchestra and I would like to start a committee to work on community orchestra budgeting strategies. In times of declining government aid for the arts, it is increasingly important that methods of containing costs and increasing nongovernmental support be found. If you are interested in working with this committee, please call me at (203)555-1312 or Susan at (914)555-9876. After we get a list of potential participants, we will try to arrange a meeting at a central location.

We thought that a good starting point would be a discussion of how we currently spend and raise money. I am including a pie chart of the Powell Community Orchestra expenses for the past year (updated to include the latest figures!). We'd be interested in knowing whether this breakdown of expenses corresponds to that of your orchestra.

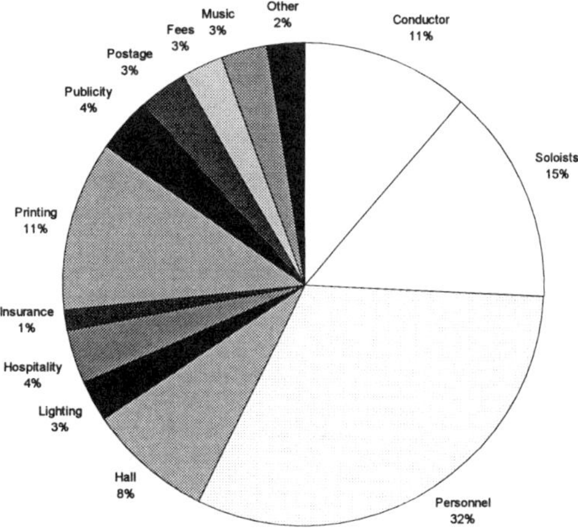

Figure 3 - 21: Completed memo

Lesson

Using *Excel* and *Access* in Mail Merge

Objectives

In this lesson you will learn how to:

- Use Word's **Mail Merge** feature with data in an *Excel* worksheet
- Use Word's **Mail Merge** feature with data in an *Access* table
- Use **Query Options** to select records in a data file for a **Mail Merge** in *Word*

PROJECT DESCRIPTION

If you have used the **Mail Merge** of *Word 6.0 for Windows*, you have seen that both the *Main Document* and the *Data Source* originate in *Word.* In this project, you will see that the data file can also be an *Excel* worksheet or an *Access* table. Thus, you will learn that you may keep your data files in *Word, Excel,* or *Access,* and still create form letters, envelopes, or labels in *Word.* The data file you will use is called **mailing**. It contains a list of subscribers to the Powell Community Orchestra, and information on when they have renewed their subscriptions. You will find the file saved as an *Excel* worksheet and a similar file saved as an *Access* table. You will write two letters, one to the subscribers who have renewed their subscriptions, thanking them for their support, and one to the subscribers who have not renewed, reminding them that the first concert is approaching, and asking them to send in a subscription renewal. There is no need for copying, pasting, linking or embedding in this project — instead, in this situation you are able to seamlessly integrate data from one application with data from another.

THE MAIL MERGE FEATURE OF WORD

As you learned in *Getting Started with Word 6.0 for Windows*, the **Mail Merge** feature of *Word for Windows* is designed to allow you to produce letters, envelopes, and labels for a group of individuals whose information is specified in a file called a **Data Source**. This data source is a *Word* table, which organizes the data in columns and rows. Each row represents the information for one individual, and each column represents a specific piece of information, for example a city or zip code. *Excel* worksheets are capable of organizing information in the same format, and so are *Access* tables. Therefore, there is no reason that data files from either of these applications cannot be used successfully with the **Mail Merge** feature.

We will present the steps for producing two sets of form letters, one using an *Excel* worksheet as the data file and one using an *Access* table. The data files you will use have been prepared for you. If you find the activities difficult, please refer to *Getting Started with Word 6.0 for Windows*, which offers a full explanation of the **Mail Merge** feature.

Activity 4.1: Setting up a Mail Merge with an Excel Data Source

In this activity, you will use the **Mail Merge Helper** to set up a merge so that you can create form letters. The Main Document will be created in *Word*, and the Data File will come from *Excel*.

1. Open Microsoft Office and open *Excel*.
2. Open the file from your data disk called **mailing.xls**.
3. Look over the file and note the information it contains, including the field called **Date Ren**, which contains the date of subscription renewal, and the field called **Since**, which contains the year that the individual first subscribed to the orchestra's concerts.

4. Change the **Zoom** percentage to **85%** so that you can see the entire file at once (Figure 4 - 1).

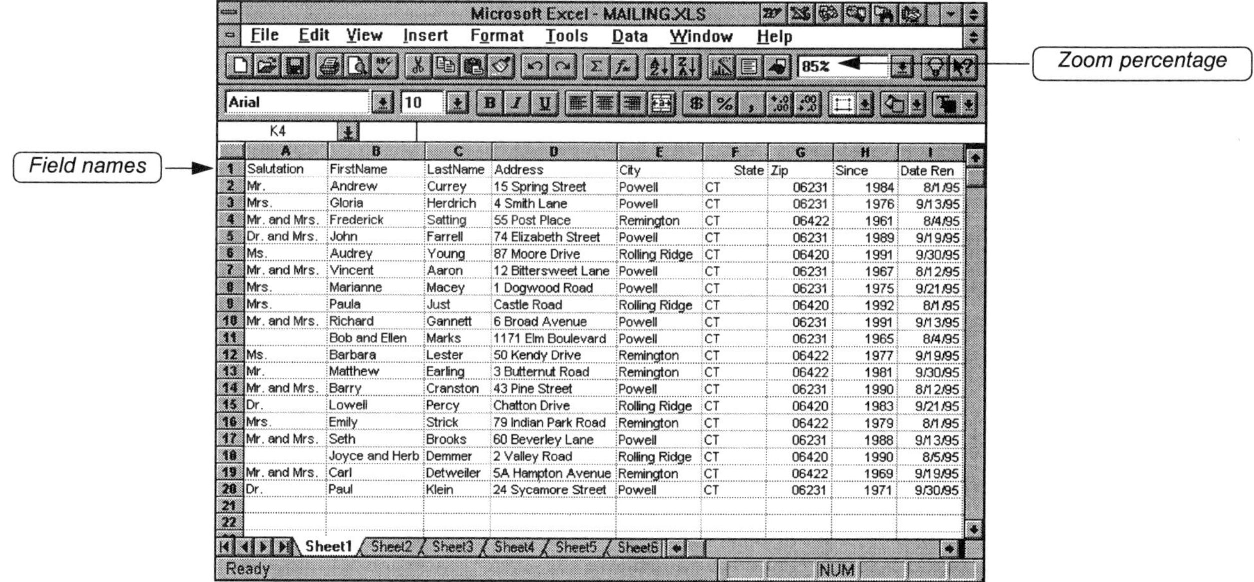

	A	B	C	D	E	F	G	H	I
1	Salutation	FirstName	LastName	Address	City	State	Zip	Since	Date Ren
2	Mr.	Andrew	Currey	15 Spring Street	Powell	CT	06231	1984	8/1/95
3	Mrs.	Gloria	Herdrich	4 Smith Lane	Powell	CT	06231	1976	9/13/95
4	Mr. and Mrs.	Frederick	Satting	55 Post Place	Remington	CT	06422	1961	8/4/95
5	Dr. and Mrs.	John	Farrell	74 Elizabeth Street	Powell	CT	06231	1989	9/19/95
6	Ms.	Audrey	Young	87 Moore Drive	Rolling Ridge	CT	06420	1991	9/30/95
7	Mr. and Mrs.	Vincent	Aaron	12 Bittersweet Lane	Powell	CT	06231	1967	8/12/95
8	Mrs.	Marianne	Macey	1 Dogwood Road	Powell	CT	06231	1975	9/21/95
9	Mrs.	Paula	Just	Castle Road	Rolling Ridge	CT	06420	1992	8/1/95
10	Mr. and Mrs.	Richard	Gannett	6 Broad Avenue	Powell	CT	06231	1991	9/13/95
11		Bob and Ellen	Marks	1171 Elm Boulevard	Powell	CT	06231	1965	8/4/95
12	Ms.	Barbara	Lester	50 Kendy Drive	Remington	CT	06422	1977	9/19/95
13	Mr.	Matthew	Earling	3 Butternut Road	Remington	CT	06422	1981	9/30/95
14	Mr. and Mrs.	Barry	Cranston	43 Pine Street	Powell	CT	06231	1990	8/12/95
15	Dr.	Lowell	Percy	Chatton Drive	Rolling Ridge	CT	06420	1983	9/21/95
16	Mrs.	Emily	Strick	79 Indian Park Road	Remington	CT	06422	1979	8/1/95
17	Mr. and Mrs.	Seth	Brooks	60 Beverley Lane	Powell	CT	06231	1988	9/13/95
18		Joyce and Herb	Demmer	2 Valley Road	Rolling Ridge	CT	06420	1990	8/5/95
19	Mr. and Mrs.	Carl	Detweiler	5A Hampton Avenue	Remington	CT	06422	1969	9/19/95
20	Dr.	Paul	Klein	24 Sycamore Street	Powell	CT	06231	1971	9/30/95
21									
22									

Figure 4 - 1

5. Close the file and close *Excel.*
6. Open *Word* and begin a new document.
7. At the menu, choose **TOOLS/Mail Merge**.
8. Choose **Create** and **Form Letters**.
9. Choose **Active Window**.
10. Choose **Get Data** and **Open Data Source**.
11. Change to the drive containing your data disk.
12. At the **List Files of Type** box choose **MS Excel Worksheets (*.xls)** (Figure 4 - 2).
13. Choose **mailing.xls** and **OK**.
14. Choose **Entire Spreadsheet** and **OK** on the next dialog box that appears.

    *An **Alert** box stating that there are no merge fields in your document appears.*

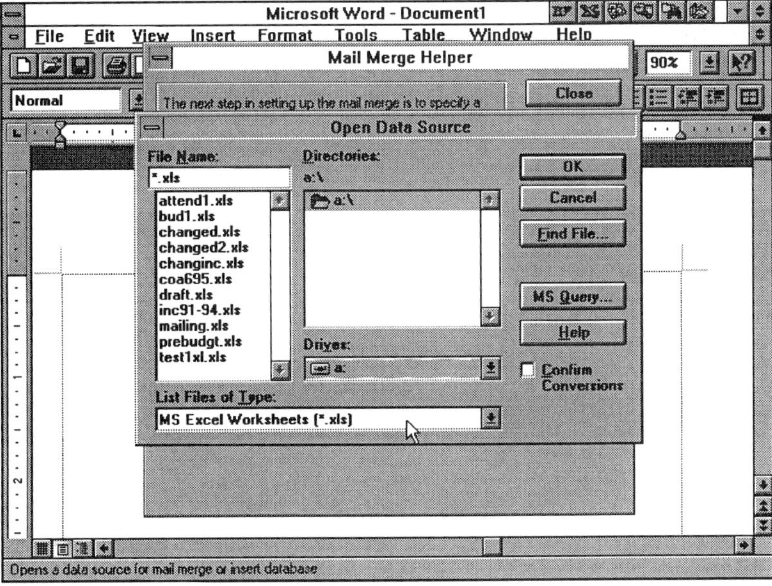

Figure 4 - 2 Changing the File Type

15. Choose **Edit Main Document**.

    Notice that the Mail Merge toolbar has been added to your Word screen. The first button on the toolbar, ***Insert Merge Field****, contains all the fields from the Excel worksheet. You can insert these fields into your Main Document, just as if they came from a Word data file.*

    Excel and the worksheet ***mailing.xls*** *opened automatically when you chose it as your Data Source. If you click on the Excel button on the Office toolbar you will see that the worksheet is displayed. Click on the Word button on the toolbar to return to Word.*

16. Change the top margin to 3", using **FILE/Page Setup**.
17. At the top of the Main Document, type the following date: **October 5, 1995**
18. Press **ENTER** twice.
19. Click on the **INSERT MERGE FIELD** button and choose **Salutation** (Figure 4 - 3).

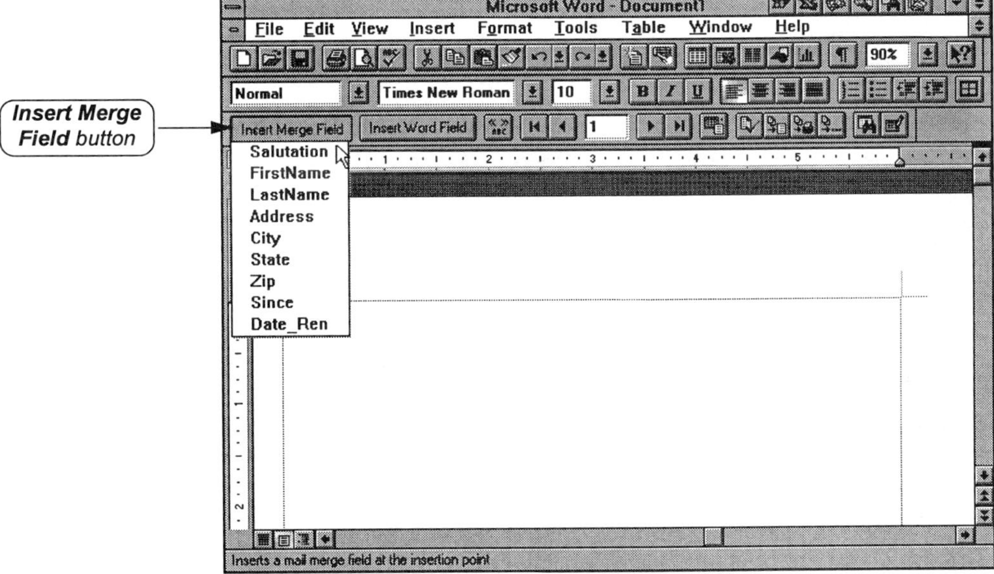

Figure 4 - 3 Inserting a Merge Field

20. Continue to add fields, using the **INSERT MERGE FIELD** button until your document looks like the following. Don't forget to add spaces and punctuation between fields.

    <<Salutation>> <<FirstName>> <<LastName>>
    <<Address>>
    <<City>>, <<State>> <<Zip>>

    Dear <<Salutation>> <<LastName>>:

21. Press **ENTER** twice and type the body of the letter as follows. Notice that one more field is included.

    Thank you for renewing your subscription to the Powell Community Orchestra. You have been a member of our organization since <<Since>>, and we recognize and appreciate your support.

    We have planned an exciting new season, beginning with our opening concert on October 28th, when Adam Marrani, concertmaster of the Milan Symphony, will be our soloist in Vivaldi's *Four Seasons*. After the concert, please join us at a reception in the atrium to greet Sr. Marrani and members of the orchestra.

    We look forward to seeing you.

    Sincerely,

    (Type your name here)
    Membership Chairman

22. Save the file as **renew.doc**. Your file will resemble Figure 4 - 4.

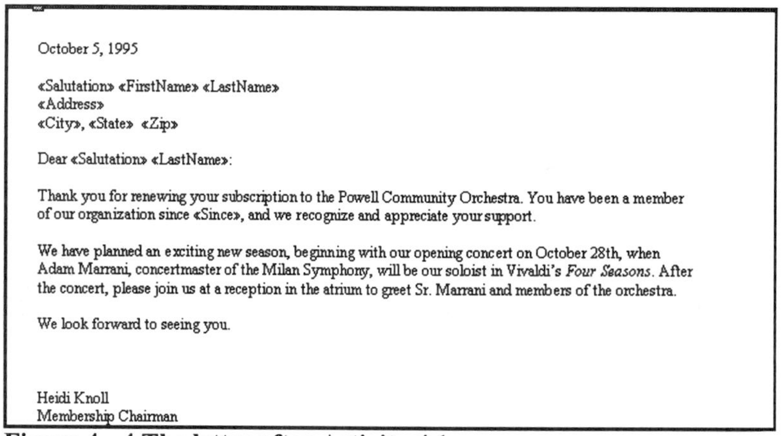

October 5, 1995

«Salutation» «FirstName» «LastName»
«Address»
«City», «State» «Zip»

Dear «Salutation» «LastName»:

Thank you for renewing your subscription to the Powell Community Orchestra. You have been a member of our organization since «Since», and we recognize and appreciate your support.

We have planned an exciting new season, beginning with our opening concert on October 28th, when Adam Marrani, concertmaster of the Milan Symphony, will be our soloist in Vivaldi's *Four Seasons*. After the concert, please join us at a reception in the atrium to greet Sr. Marrani and members of the orchestra.

We look forward to seeing you.

Heidi Knoll
Membership Chairman

Figure 4 - 4 The letter after Activity 4.1

Activity 4.2: Merging the Files

There are several ways in which you can merge the files. You can return to the Mail Merge Helper and choose its **Merge** command. This enables you to merge all the records in the data file or to merge selectively, setting up criteria for the records you want included in the merge. You can also merge the files by clicking on one of the buttons on the **Mail Merge** toolbar, **MERGE TO PRINTER,** or **MERGE TO NEW DOCUMENT**. You will merge directly to a new document in this activity.

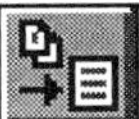

1. Point to the **Mail Merge** toolbar until you see the button marked **MERGE TO NEW DOCUMENT** and click (Figure 4 - 5).

   *It will take a moment or two until the merge is complete. The merged document will have the temporary name **Form Letters1**.*

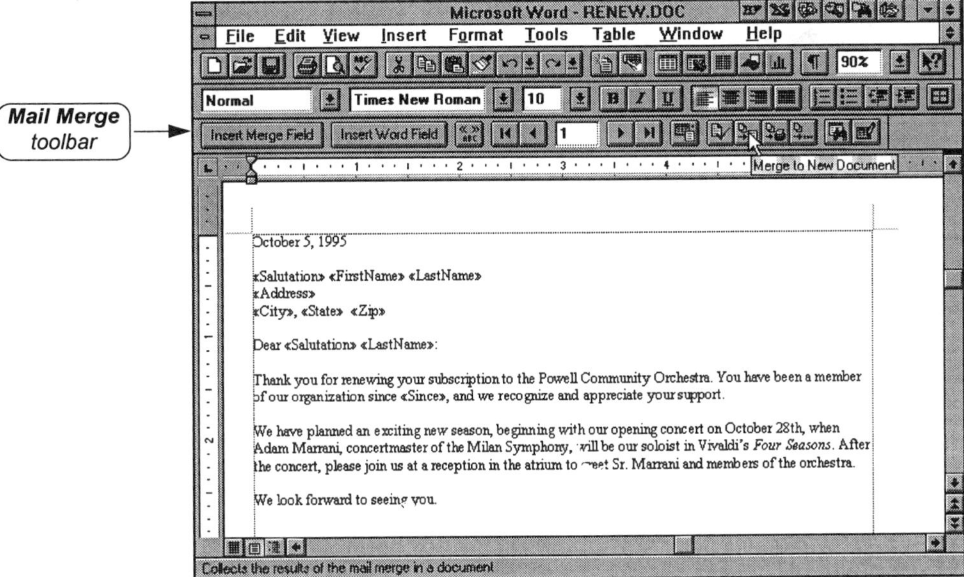

Figure 4 - 5 Choosing Merge to New Document

2. Scroll the document and examine the first two or three letters. Notice how the text of the letter remains the same. Only the data fields from *Excel* contain different information.
3. Click on the **Excel** button on the Office toolbar. Notice that the data file is still open.
4. Click on the **Word** button to return to *Word*.
5. Print Page **1** of the **Form Letters** document.
6. Save the file of form letters as **renthanx.doc**. Your document will resemble Figure 4 - 6.

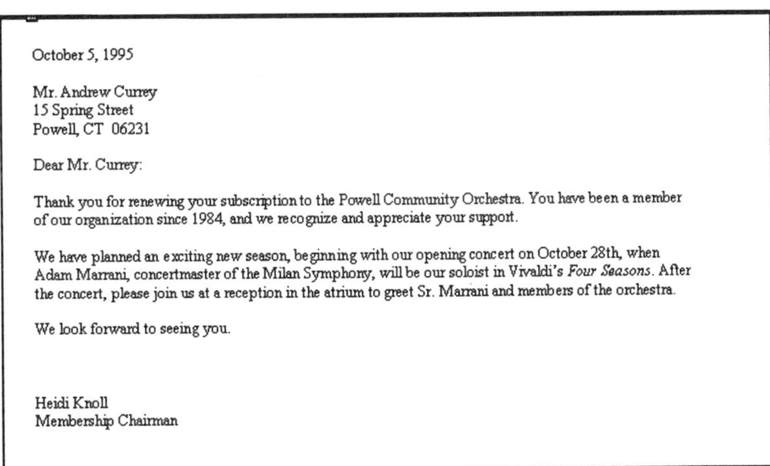

October 5, 1995

Mr. Andrew Currey
15 Spring Street
Powell, CT 06231

Dear Mr. Currey:

Thank you for renewing your subscription to the Powell Community Orchestra. You have been a member of our organization since 1984, and we recognize and appreciate your support.

We have planned an exciting new season, beginning with our opening concert on October 28th, when Adam Marrani, concertmaster of the Milan Symphony, will be our soloist in Vivaldi's *Four Seasons*. After the concert, please join us at a reception in the atrium to greet Sr. Marrani and members of the orchestra.

We look forward to seeing you.

Heidi Knoll
Membership Chairman

Figure 4 - 6 One of the letters after Activity 4.2

7. Close **renthanx.doc**.

*You will return to **renew.doc**.*

8. Close **renew.doc**.

   Closing this document also closes Excel because closing the Main Document closes the Data Source and its application.

Using Access files with Word

There are more similarities than differences between using an *Excel* file and an *Access* table as a Data Source. In this activity, you will use a similar, but not identical, data file that contains individuals who have renewed as well as individuals who have *not* renewed their subscriptions to the orchestra. Your letter will address only those who have not renewed. There are several ways in which to select only the records of subscribers who have not renewed. One way is to use an *Access* Query to find those individuals and use the Query results as the Data Source. Another way is to use the entire *Access* table as a Data Source but merge only the records of the subscribers who have not renewed. This is the method you will follow in Activity 4.3.

Activity 4.3: Setting up a Mail Merge with an Access Data Source

1. Open *Word*, if it is not already running.
2. Begin a new document.
3. Choose **TOOLS/Mail Merge,Create** and **Form Letters**.
4. Choose **Active Window**.
5. Choose **Get Data/Open Data source**.
6. At the box marked **List Files of Type**, choose **MS Access Databases (*.mdb)**.
7. Choose the database called **office.mdb** and click on **OK** (Figure 4 - 7).

   *A dialog box will open that contains a list of tables and queries. Either a table or a query may be used as a Data Source for Word's Mail Merge. You will use the table called **mailing**.*

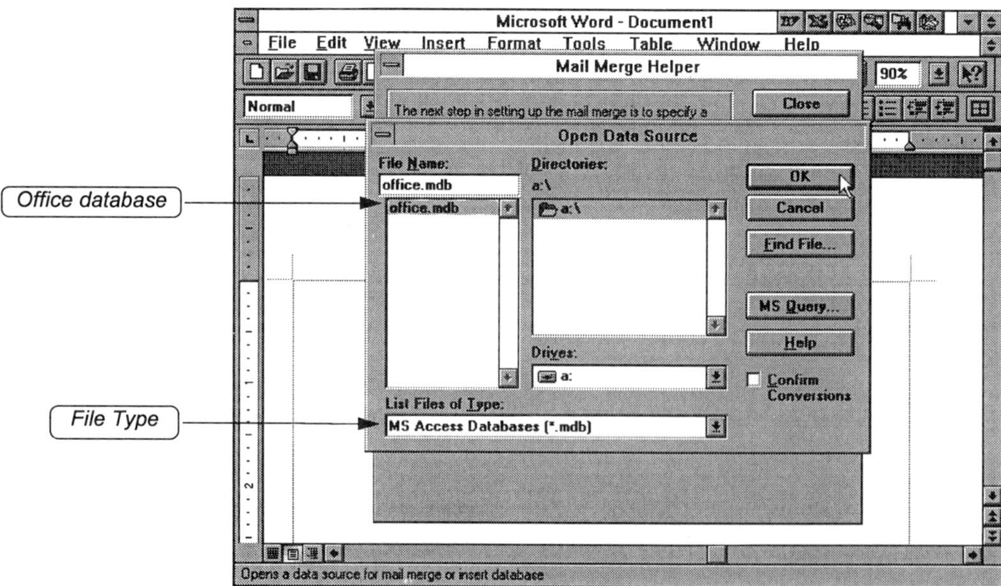

Figure 4 - 7 Choosing an Access file as a Data Source

8. Choose **Mailing** and **OK**.

9. Choose **Edit Main Document**.

   *The situation is almost identical to the one you encountered when Excel data was used. Access has been opened automatically, as well as the table you chose (**mailing**).*

10. Change the top margin to 3".

11. Type the date: **October 5, 1995**

12. Press **ENTER** twice.

13. Again, use the **INSERT MERGE FIELD** button on the **Mail Merge** toolbar to create the beginning of your file as follows:

    <<Salutation>> <<FirstName>> <<LastName>>
    <<Address>>
    <<City>>, <<State>> <<Zip>>

    Dear <<Salutation>> <<LastName>>:

14. Press **ENTER** twice and type the body of the letter as follows:

    Our records show that you have not yet renewed your subscription to the Powell Community Orchestra for 1995 - 1996. We hope this is an oversight and that you will be sending in your renewal form shortly.

    You have been a subscriber to the orchestra since <<Since>>, and we value and appreciate your support. It is our loyal base of subscribers that has enabled us to bring concerts of the highest quality to our community for so many years.

    As you saw in our subscription brochure, our first concert of the season, which will take place on October 28th, features Adam Marrani of the Milan Symphony playing Vivaldi's *Four Seasons*. We hope you will be there to enjoy the evening.

    Sincerely yours,

    (Type your name here)
    Membership Chairman

15. Save the file as **nonrenew.doc**. Your file will resemble Figure 4 - 8.

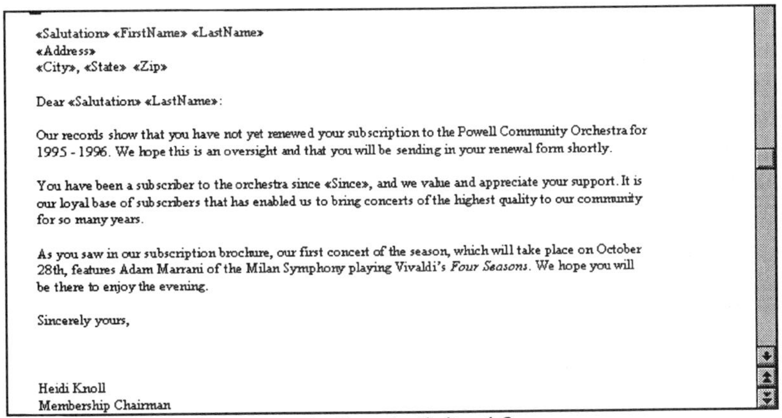

«Salutation» «FirstName» «LastName»
«Address»
«City», «State» «Zip»

Dear «Salutation» «LastName»:

Our records show that you have not yet renewed your subscription to the Powell Community Orchestra for 1995 - 1996. We hope this is an oversight and that you will be sending in your renewal form shortly.

You have been a subscriber to the orchestra since «Since», and we value and appreciate your support. It is our loyal base of subscribers that has enabled us to bring concerts of the highest quality to our community for so many years.

As you saw in our subscription brochure, our first concert of the season, which will take place on October 28th, features Adam Marrani of the Milan Symphony playing Vivaldi's *Four Seasons*. We hope you will be there to enjoy the evening.

Sincerely yours,

Heidi Knoll
Membership Chairman

Figure 4 - 8 The Document after Activity 4.3

Activity 4.4: Merging Access and Word Files

You are going to merge the letter you just created, **nonrenew.doc**, with the data file from *Access*. Since the letter will be mailed to the subscribers who have not yet renewed, you will first examine the table and notice those subscribers. Then, you will merge only the records of those subscribers with the *Word* letter.

1. Click on the **Access** button on the Office toolbar.

   In the directory that contains your data files, you will see the listing for the table called ***mailing****.*

   PROBLEM SOLVER: *If there is no Access button on the Office toolbar, click on the Microsoft Office button and click on Microsoft Access.*

2. Select **mailing** and choose the **Open** button.
3. Maximize the *Access* window and the Table window.
4. Scroll the table to the right until the column marked **Date Ren** is showing (Figure 4 - 9).

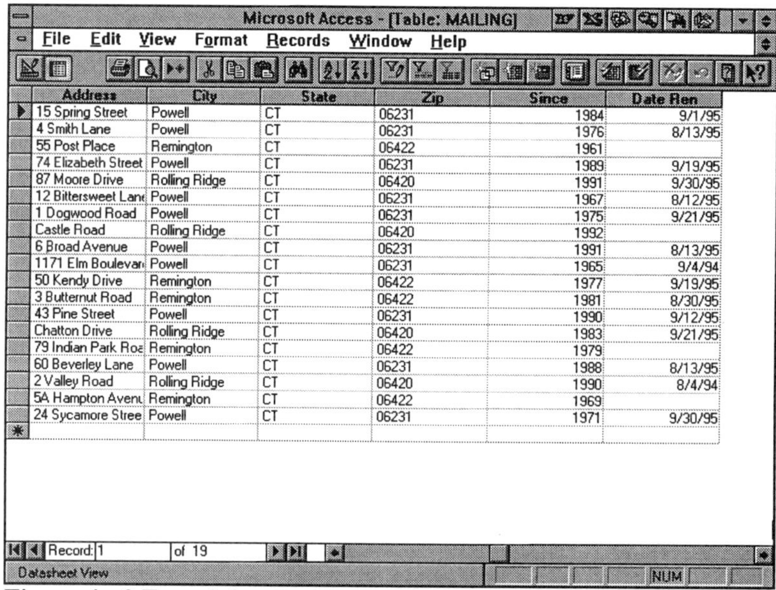

Address	City	State	Zip	Since	Date Ren
15 Spring Street	Powell	CT	06231	1984	9/1/95
4 Smith Lane	Powell	CT	06231	1976	8/13/95
55 Post Place	Remington	CT	06422	1961	
74 Elizabeth Street	Powell	CT	06231	1989	9/19/95
87 Moore Drive	Rolling Ridge	CT	06420	1991	9/30/95
12 Bittersweet Lane	Powell	CT	06231	1967	8/12/95
1 Dogwood Road	Powell	CT	06231	1975	9/21/95
Castle Road	Rolling Ridge	CT	06420	1992	
6 Broad Avenue	Powell	CT	06231	1991	8/13/95
1171 Elm Boulevar	Powell	CT	06231	1965	9/4/94
50 Kendy Drive	Remington	CT	06422	1977	9/19/95
3 Butternut Road	Remington	CT	06422	1981	8/30/95
43 Pine Street	Powell	CT	06231	1990	9/12/95
Chatton Drive	Rolling Ridge	CT	06420	1983	9/21/95
79 Indian Park Roa	Remington	CT	06422	1979	
60 Beverley Lane	Powell	CT	06231	1988	8/13/95
2 Valley Road	Rolling Ridge	CT	06420	1990	8/4/94
5A Hampton Avenu	Remington	CT	06422	1969	
24 Sycamore Stree	Powell	CT	06231	1971	9/30/95

Figure 4 - 9 Examining the Date Renewed Field in the Access Table

   Notice the blank lines in the last column. Any entry that is blank represents a subscriber who has not renewed. A total of 4 records are blank. Scrolling back and forth, you can see that the names of the subscribers who have not renewed are ***Satting, Just, Strick, and Detweiler****.*

5. Close the table but do not close *Access*.
6. Click on the **Word** button to return to your letter.

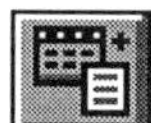

7. Point to the **Mail Merge** toolbar until you see the button marked **Mail Merge Helper** button and click (Figure 4 - 10).

   Notice how the ***Mail Merge Helper*** *box has been filled in. You will see the type of merge (****Form Letters****), the name of the Main Document (****nonrenew.doc****), and the name of the Data Source (****office.mdb!table mailing****).*

8. Since you do not want to merge all records, choose the button at the bottom of the box marked **Query Options**.

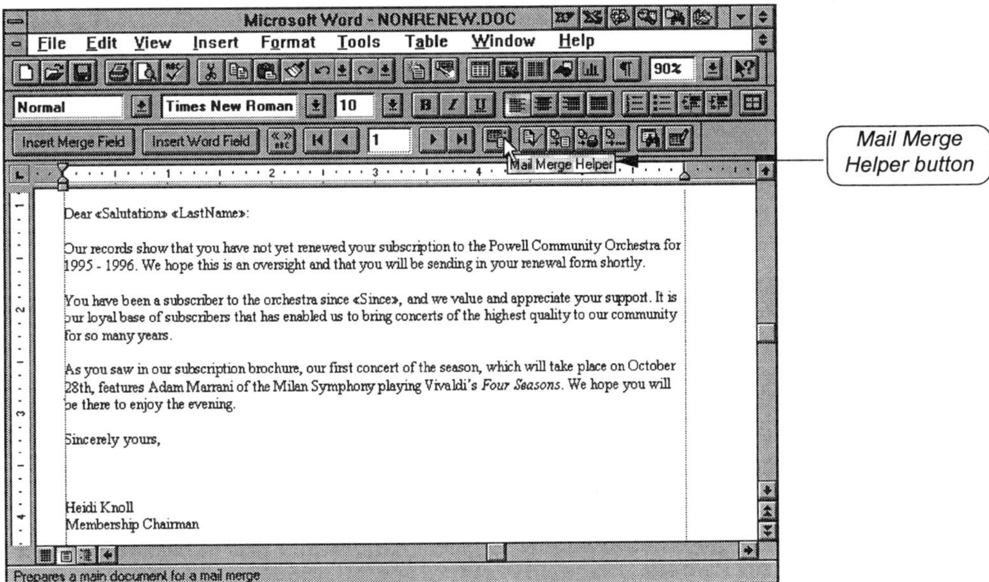

Figure 4 - 10 Returning to the Mail Merge Helper

9. Open the list under the word **Field:** and choose **Date Ren**.

   This means that you will be examining the data in that field.

10. Open the list under the word **Comparison:** and choose **is Blank** (Figure 4 - 11).

    This means that in order to be included in the merge, this field must be blank in the data file.

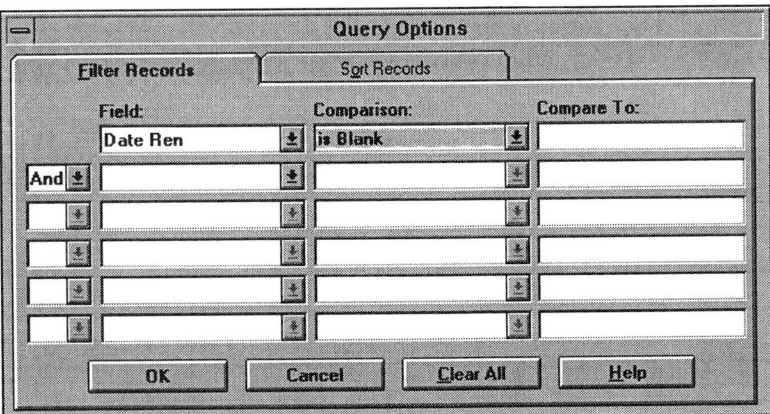

Figure 4 - 11 The Completed Query Options Box

11. Choose **OK** to return to the **Mail Merge Helper**.
12. Click on the button marked **Merge**.
13. At the next box, again click on the button marked **Merge**.

    *You will see the merged document, again called **Form Letters**. This time the Status Bar will tell you that the document consists of 4 pages, representing the 4 records with no entry in the **Date Ren** column.*

14. Scroll the file and note the name on each letter (**Satting, Just, Strick,** and **Detweiler**), the same names you saw when you examined the *Access* table. The first page of your document should resemble Figure 4 - 12.

October 5, 1995

Mr. and Mrs. Frederick Satting
55 Post Place
Remington, CT 06422

Dear Mr. and Mrs. Satting:

Our records show that you have not yet renewed your subscription to the Powell Community Orchestra for 1995 - 1996. We hope this is an oversight and that you will be sending in your renewal form shortly.

You have been a subscriber to the orchestra since 1961, and we value and appreciate your support. It is our loyal base of subscribers that has enabled us to bring concerts of the highest quality to our community for so many years.

As you saw in our subscription brochure, our first concert of the season, which will take place on October 28th, features Adam Marrani of the Milan Symphony playing Vivaldi's *Four Seasons*. We hope you will be there to enjoy the evening.

Sincerely yours,

Heidi Knoll
Membership Chairman

Figure 4 - 12 Page 1 of the Form Letters

15. Print the entire document.
16. Close the file of form letters without saving.
17. Close the other files that are open and exit from *Word.*

SUMMARY

In this lesson, you have learned to use Word's Mail Merge feature using Data Source files from *Excel* and then from *Access.* Both these applications offer data in tabular form, which is easily read by *Word.* Neither linking nor embedding is necessary to share data for purposes of Mail Merge.

KEY TERMS

Comparison
Data File
Data Source
Form Letters
Insert Merge Field button
Mail Merge
Main Document
Merge to New Document
Query Options

INDEPENDENT PROJECTS

Independent Project 4.1: Using a Data Source from Excel in Mail Merge

In this project, the Powell Community Orchestra is planning a Winter Ball to raise money for the following season. An *Excel* worksheet holds information about caterers, florists and other merchants to be contacted. You will use this worksheet as the Data Source for a Mail Merge, creating form letters to these individuals.

1. Open *Word for Windows.*
2. Choose **TOOLS/Mail Merge**.
3. Choose **Create** and **Form Letters**.
4. Choose **Active Window**.
5. Choose **Get Data** and **Open Data Source**.
6. Change to the drive containing your data disk.
7. At the **List Files of Type** box, choose **MS Excel Worksheets (*.xls)**.

8. Choose **winball.xls** and choose **OK**.
9. Choose **Entire Spreadsheet** and **OK**.
10. Choose **Edit Main Document**.
11. Change the top margin to 2.5" to leave room for the orchestra letterhead.
12. Type the following date: **June 30, 1995** and press **ENTER** twice.
13. Use the **Insert Merge Field** button to insert the following fields:

    <<Salutation>> <<FirstName>> <<LastName>>
    <<Company>>
    <<Address>>
    <<City>>, <<State>> <<Zip>>

    Dear <<Salutation>> <<LastName>>:

14. Type the body of the letter as follows:

    The Powell Community Orchestra is beginning to plan its Winter Ball, which will take place next December 2, 1995. This ball will be our major fundraising activity for the year, and the proceeds will be used to help defray the costs of our 1996 - 1997 concert season.

    We would like to know if you would like to help us by donating goods and/or services for the ball. We will be seeking food, flowers, printing services, and gift certificates to be used as door prizes from area merchants.

    A representative from our committee will be contacting you within the next few weeks to discuss the ball. We hope you will join our many friends in the community who will be helping us.

    Sincerely,

    Greta Kornreich, Chairperson
    Winter Ball Committee

15. Save the letter as **merchant.doc**.
16. Click on the **Merge to New Document** button on the Database Toolbar.
17. Check the letters.
18. Print the letter to Joseph Felton.
19. Do not save the file of form letters.
20. Close **merchant.doc** and exit from *Word.*

Independent Project 4.2: Using a Data Source from Access in Mail Merge

As the Winter Ball approaches, the Powell Community orchestra is sending a thank you letter to major donors. The donors have purchased an entire table of tickets ($800) to the ball. You will use a Data Source from *Access* which has information on many donors, but you will send letters only to those who have bought a full table.

1. Open *Word for Windows*.
2. Choose **TOOLS/Mail Merge**.

3. Choose **Create** and **Form Letters**.
4. Choose **Active Window**.
5. Choose **Get Data** and **Open Data Source**.
6. Change to the drive containing your data disk.
7. At the **List Files of Type** box, choose **MS Access Databases (*.mdb)**.
8. Choose **office.mdb** and **OK.**
9. At the **Tables** section of the **Microsoft Access** dialog box, choose **donors** and **OK**.
10. Choose **Edit Main Document**.
11. Change the top margin to 2.5" to leave room for the orchestra letterhead.
12. Type the following date: **November 1, 1995** and press **ENTER** twice.
13. Use the **Insert Merge Field** button to insert the following fields:

    <<Salutation>> <<FirstName>> <<LastName>>
    <<Address>>
    <<City>>, <<State>> <<Zip>>

    Dear <<Salutation>> <<LastName>>:
14. Type the body of the letter as follows:

    On behalf of the Board of Trustees of the Powell Community Orchestra, we would like to thank you for purchasing a table at the Winter Ball. Your generosity is helping to make the ball a success, and provide needed funding for our 1996 - 1997 season.

    As a token of our gratitude, we are sending you an autographed copy of Bernard Leiden's famous biography of Frederic Chopin.

    We look forward to seeing you and your guests at the ball.

    Sincerely,

    Greta Kornreich, Chairperson
    Winter Ball Committee
15. Save the file as **tables.doc**.
16. Use the Microsoft Office Toolbar to switch to *Access* and open the table called **Donors**.
17. Scroll the database and examine the field called **Full Table.**

    *There are three records that say **Yes**, indicating donors who have purchased a table, Record 4 (Dr. and Mrs. John Farrell), Record 10 (Bob and Ellen Marks), and Record 14 (Dr. Lowell Percy).*
18. Close the table but do not close *Access*.
19. Return to *Word*.
20. Click on the **Mail Merge Helper** button on the **Mail Merge** Toolbar.
21. Choose **Query Options**.
22. Open the list under the word **Field:** and choose **Full Table**.
23. Open the list under the word **Compare To:** and type **Yes**.
24. Choose **OK**.

25. Click on the **Merge to New Document** button on the **Mail Merge** Toolbar.
26. Examine the **Form Letters** document. It will have three pages, one for each record in *Access* that showed a donor who purchased a table.

Problem Solver: *If you see a message from Word saying:* ***Word could not parse your query options into a valid SQL string****, you have tried merging from the* ***Mail Merge Helper.*** *For this exercise, we are merging from the* ***Mail Merge*** *Toolbar. Try Step 25 again.*

27. Print the letter to Dr. Percy.
28. Do not save the Form Letters file.
29. Resave **tables.doc** and exit from *Word.*

Appendix

SYSTEMS REQUIREMENTS FOR RUNNING MICROSOFT OFFICE

Microsoft Office is a huge program, and requires more storage space and computer power than many PCs have. Do not attempt to install or run Microsoft Office unless you meet the requirements listed below. If you barely meet the minimum requirements, be prepared for the possibility of slow processing, occasional program crashes, and the chance that you will be unable to run more than one application at a time.

Minimum Requirements:

1. **DOS**: version 3.1 or later
2. **Windows**: version 3.1 or later. For running Microsoft Office on a network, Windows for Workgroups 3.1 or later, Windows NT or Windows NT Advanced Server 3.1 or later.
3. **Microprocessor**: 386 or higher
4. **Memory**: 8 MB recommended/ 4 MB required to integrate applications (to run more than one program simultaneously); with 4 MB of RAM performance will be very slow and size of open documents and number of applications opened will be limited.
5. **Hard Disk Space**: For Microsoft Office Standard, 21 MB for the minimum installation, 49 MB for a typical installation, and 68 MB for a complete installation. For Microsoft Office Professional (including Access), 29 MB for the minimum installation, 58 MB for a typical installation, and 82 MB for a complete installation.
6. **Disk Drive**: A 3 1/2" or a 5 1/4" drive (high-density only)
7. **Video**: VGA or higher
8. **Pointing Device**: Microsoft Mouse or compatible

Features Reference

Similarities between pasting and embedding objects:

- The object is part of the destination document and is saved with that document.
- The object does not change when the source data is edited and the source data does not change when the pasted or embedded object is changed.
- The file containing the pasted or embedded object is easy to transport from computer to computer because the pasted or embedded object is actually part of the file.

Similarities between embedding and linking objects:

- You use the **Copy** and **Paste Special** functions for both.
- You will see the instruction: **Double-click to edit object** on the Status Bar for both.
- All aspects of the source object (text, formatting, formulas) are present in the destination object

Differences between pasting, embedding, and linking objects:

Pasted Object	Embedded Object	Linked Object
Only the text and formatting are copied to the destination document (i.e., a pasted worksheet contains numbers in place of any formulas that were contained in the original). Formatting may be modified to conform with formatting options of the destination application.	All aspects of the original object are present in the destination document (i.e., an embedded worksheet contains all of the formulas in the original).	The source object *is* the destination object — one set of data appearing in two places, but physically present only in the source document.
Increase in file size is approximately equal to increase that would be caused by entering the formatted text directly into the document.	Increase in file size is much larger than that accounted for by the formatted text; the entire source file and all of the information needed to edit the object in the source application are stored in the destination file.	Increase in file size is much less than in embedded object. The object data is not physically placed within the destination file.
The pasted data is edited using the commands of the destination application.	The destination object is edited using the commands of the source application.	The source object is edited. The destination object is updated when or after the source is edited.
The source application does *not* need to be present in order to edit the pasted data.	The source application must be on the computer in order to edit the object.	The source application *and the source document* must be on the computer in order to edit the linked object.
The destination file contains only the part of the source file copied and pasted into it.	The destination file contains the entire source file although only the part you copied and embedded will appear.	The destination file displays the amount of the source file that has been linked, but the entire source file is available during editing.
It is easy to transport the destination file from computer to computer.	It is still easy to transport the file from computer to computer (unless the file size is larger than the floppy disk capacity).	It is difficult to transport the file to a different computer. Both the destination and source files must be moved, and the name, drive, and directory of the source file(s) cannot change.

Criteria for Choosing a Method

The table below shows the criteria (you may have) for a given task and the method(s) of sharing data which meet the criteria. To find the *best* method, see which one fits your *most important* criteria.

If:	Choose this method:
The object in the destination document *must* update when the source document changes	Linking
You expect little or no significant change in the source document, or if the change need not be reflected in the destination document	Pasting, embedding
You want to use the *destination application* to edit or format the object in the destination document	Pasting
You want to use the commands of the *source application* to edit or format the object in the destination document	Embedding, Linking
You want to make editing changes to the object which should *not* be included in the source document	Pasting, Embedding
People who will be editing the object in the destination document do not have access to the source application	Pasting
Someone other than you will have access to the destination file and they should *not* have access to the entire source file	Pasting
It is important to keep the file size as small as possible or multiple or long objects (such as graphics files) need to be included in the destination document	Linking
There are multiple objects in a file and the file needs to be transported to other systems	Pasting, Embedding

NOTE: Pasting appears to be the most frequent method in the situations listed above. However, pasting is an older technology than object linking and embedding and has limitations not evident in the table. First, pasting is often not an option; if the data to be included in the destination document cannot be edited using the tools of the destination application, the data will be automatically embedded rather than pasted. Second, since the data is changed to a format native to the destination application, some of the original formatting may be distorted.

Index

L

M

N

O

P

R

S

T

U

V

W

Y